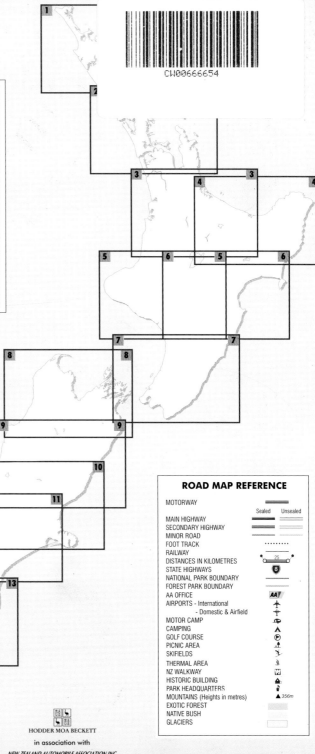

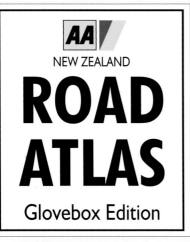

AA

NEW ZEALAND

ROAD
ATLAS

Glovebox Edition

Scale
1cm = 8.1 km

ROAD MAP REFERENCE

	Sealed	Unsealed
MOTORWAY		
MAIN HIGHWAY		
SECONDARY HIGHWAY		
MINOR ROAD		
FOOT TRACK		
RAILWAY		
DISTANCES IN KILOMETRES	25	
STATE HIGHWAYS	8	
NATIONAL PARK BOUNDARY		
FOREST PARK BOUNDARY		
AA OFFICE	AA	
AIRPORTS - International	✈	
- Domestic & Airfield	✈	
MOTOR CAMP		
CAMPING	Λ	
GOLF COURSE	℗	
PICNIC AREA	⊥	
SKIFIELDS	🎿	
THERMAL AREA	⚲	
NZ WALKWAY	W	
HISTORIC BUILDING	♙	
PARK HEADQUARTERS	♙	
MOUNTAINS (Heights in metres)	▲ 356m	
EXOTIC FOREST		
NATIVE BUSH		
GLACIERS		

HODDER MOA BECKETT

in association with

NEW ZEALAND AUTOMOBILE ASSOCIATION INC

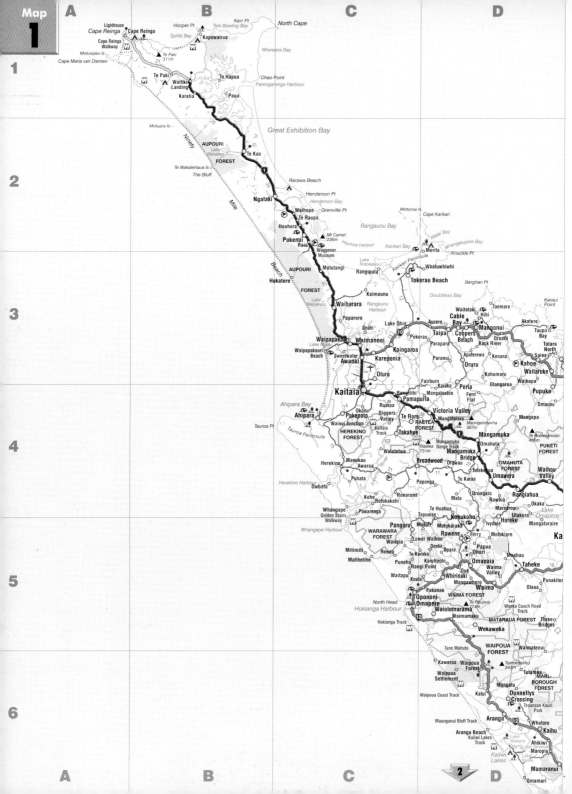

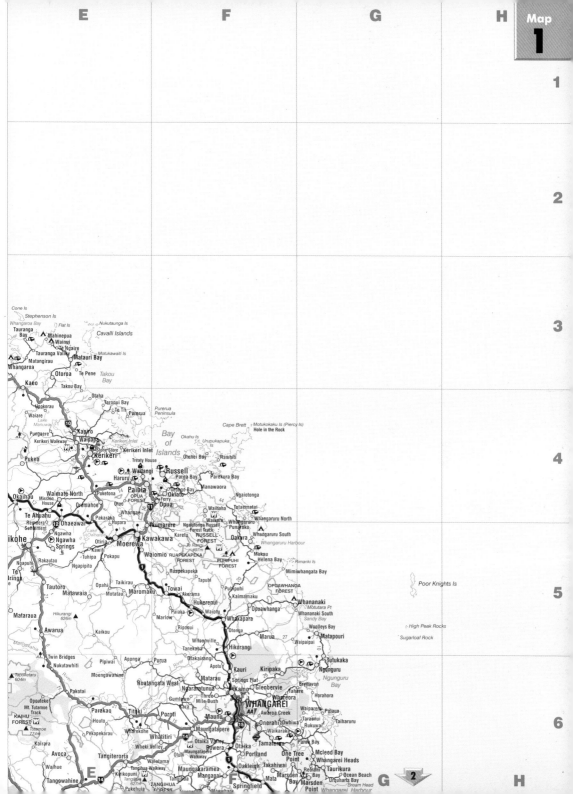

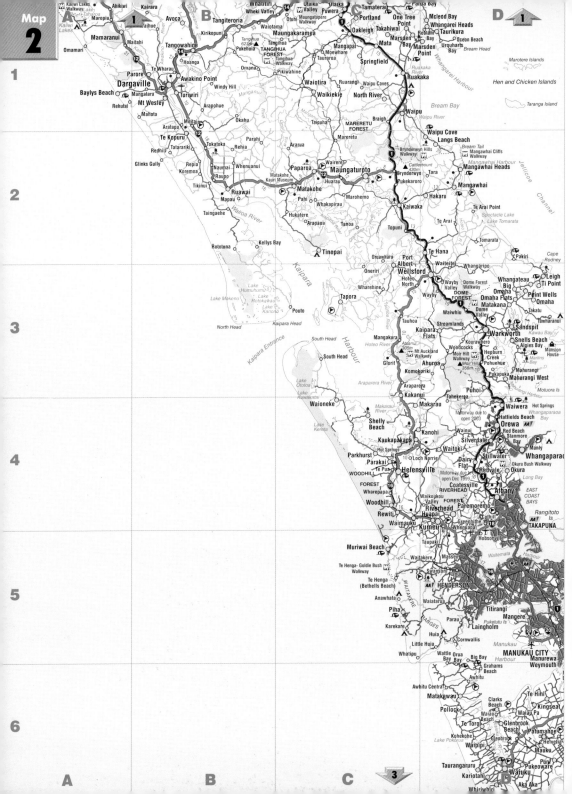

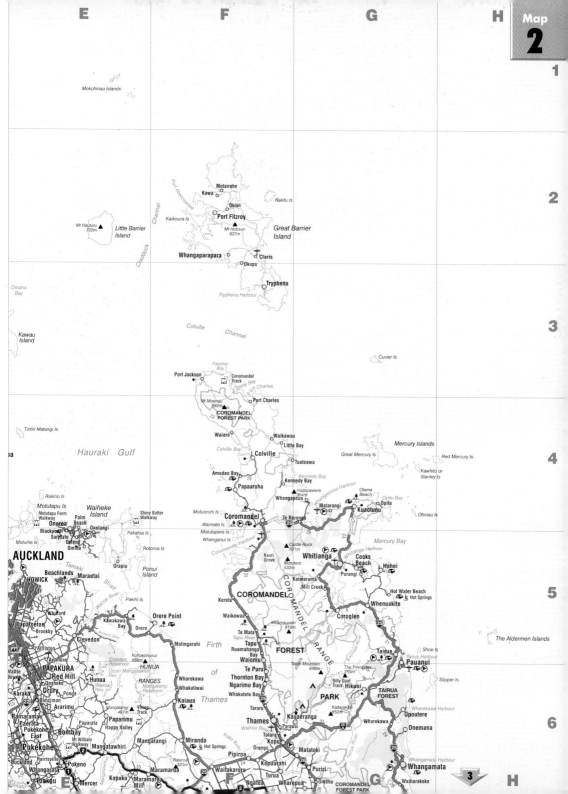

Map

2

E F G H

1

2

Mokohinau Islands

Port Abercrombie

Motairehe
Kawa
Okiwi
Rakitu Is
Kaikoura Is
Port Fitzroy
Craddock Channel
Mt Hauturu 722m ▲
Little Barrier Island
Mt Hobson 627m ▲
Great Barrier Island
Whangaparapara
✠ Claris
Okupu
Tryphena
Omaha Bay
Tryphena Harbour

3

Kawau Island
Colville Channel
Cuvier Is
Fletcher Bay
Port Jackson
Coromandel Track
Stony Bay
Charles
Port Charles
Mt Moehau 892m ▲
COROMANDEL FOREST PARK
Tiritiri Matangi Is
Waiaro
Waikawau
Little Bay
Colville Bay
Colville
Tuateawa
Mercury Islands
Great Mercury Is
Red Mercury Is

4

Hauraki Gulf
Amodeo Bay
Papaaroha
Kennedy Bay
Hapaipawera
Whangapoua
Hauraki 364m
Matarangi
Kuaotunu
Otama Beach
Opito
Opito Bay
Ohinau Is
Kawhitu or Stanley Is
Rakino Is
Motutapu Is
Waiheke Island
Motutapu Farm Walkway
Stony Batter Walkway
Palm Beach
Onetangi
Motuoruhi Is
Coromandel
Te Rerenga
Whangaoua Harbour
AUCKLAND
Onaroa
Blackpool
Surfdale
Ostend
Omiha
Pakatoa Is
Waimate Is
Motutapere Is
Whanganui Is
Coromandel Harbour
Castle Rock 521m
Motutere 532m
Whitianga
Cooks Beach
Hahei
Mercury Bay

5

Motuihe Is
Ponui Island
Rotoroa Is
Orapiu
Pakihi Is
Kauri Grove
Purangi
Kaimarama
Mill Creek
Hot Water Beach
Hot Springs
Whenuakite
Beachlands
HOWICK
Maraetai
Whitford
Brookby
Papatoetoe
Kawakawa Bay
Orere
Orere Point
Matingarahi
Firth
Waikawau
COROMANDEL
Kereta
COROMANDEL RANGE
Malumapaki 819m
Coroglen
The Aldermen Islands
Shoe Is
Clevedon
Ardmore
Alfriston
Cosseys Reservoir
Kohtkohunui 688m
Te Mata
Tapu
Ruamahanga Bay
Waiomu
FOREST
Table Mountain 846m
Tairua
Tairua Harbour
Pauanui

6

Wattle Downs
PAPAKURA
Red Hill
Hunua
Opaheke
HUNUA
Upper Mangatawhiri Res
of
Wharekawa
Whakatiwai
Te Puru
Thornton Bay
Ngarimu Bay
Whakatete Bay
The Pinnacles 759m
Billy Goat Track
Hikuai
PARK
TAIRUA FOREST
Slipper Is
Karaka
Drury
Ponga
Huncianu
Ararimu
RANGES
Mangatangi 487m
Viking Track
Kaiaua
Thames
Taruru
Kauaeranga
Kaitarakihi 652m
Wharekawa
Opoutere
Wharekawa Harbour
Onemana
Ramarama
Paerata
Pukekohe East
Paparata
Happy Valley
Papariru
Miranda
Hot Springs
Thames
Parawai
Totara
Kopu
Matatoki
Wharekawa
Bombay
Mt William Walkway
Mangatawhiri
Mangatangi
Pipiroa
Orango
Puriri
Pukekohe
Harrisville
Pokeno
Waitakaruru
Kopuarahi
Turua
Whenuakite
Whangamata
Buckland
Whangarata
Mercer
Maramarua
Maramarua Mill
Ngatea
Wharepoa
Omahu
COROMANDEL FOREST PARK
Whangamata Harbour
Waiharakeke
Tuakau
Kopuku
Piako River
Waihou River

E F G H

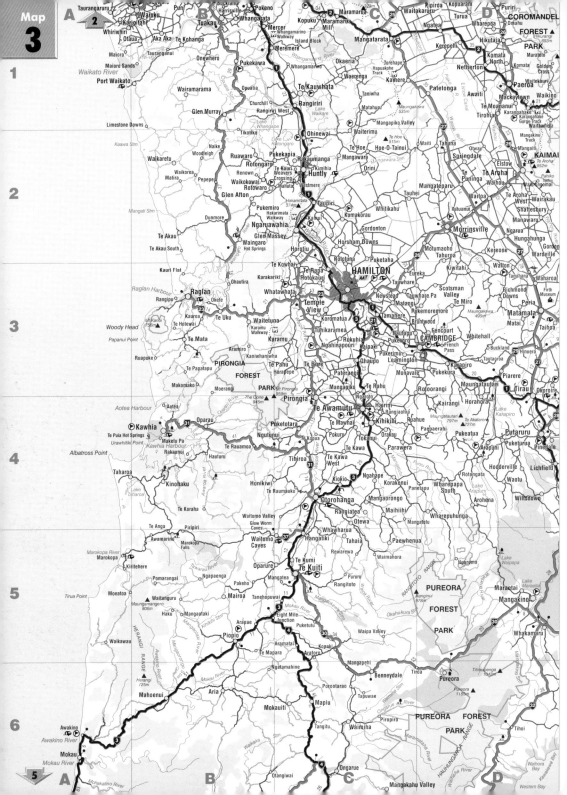

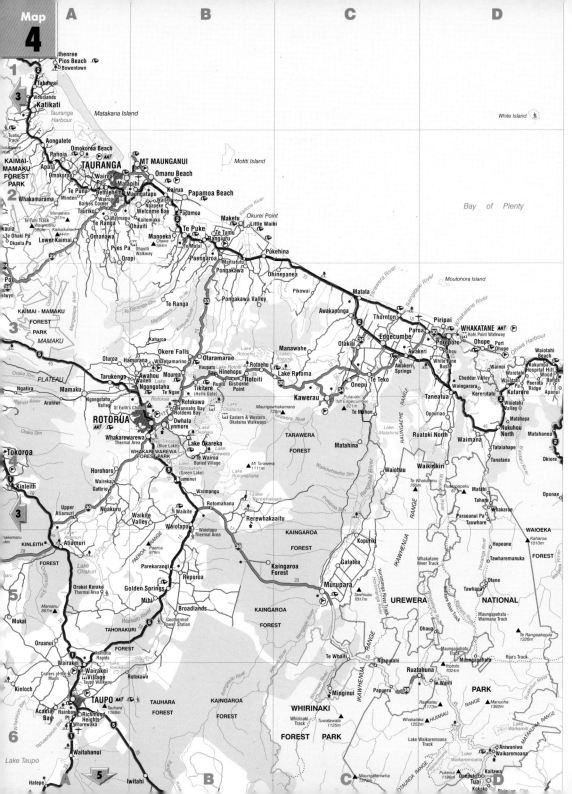

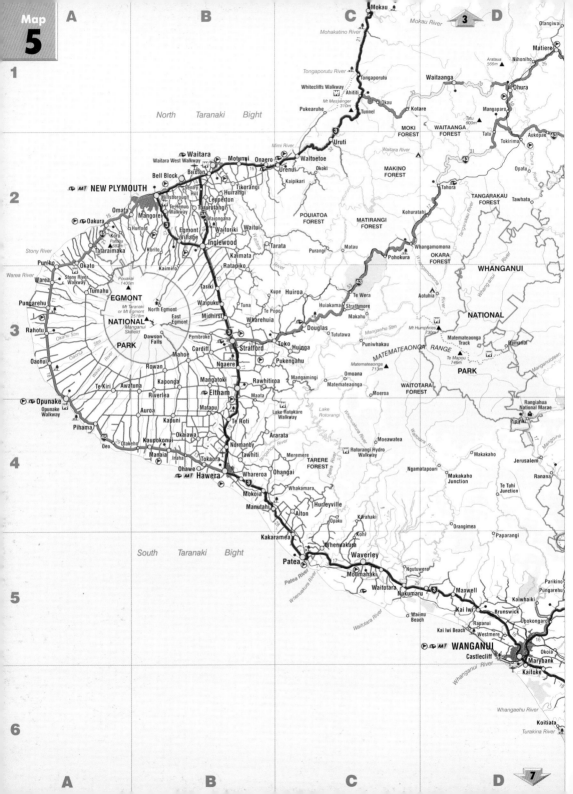

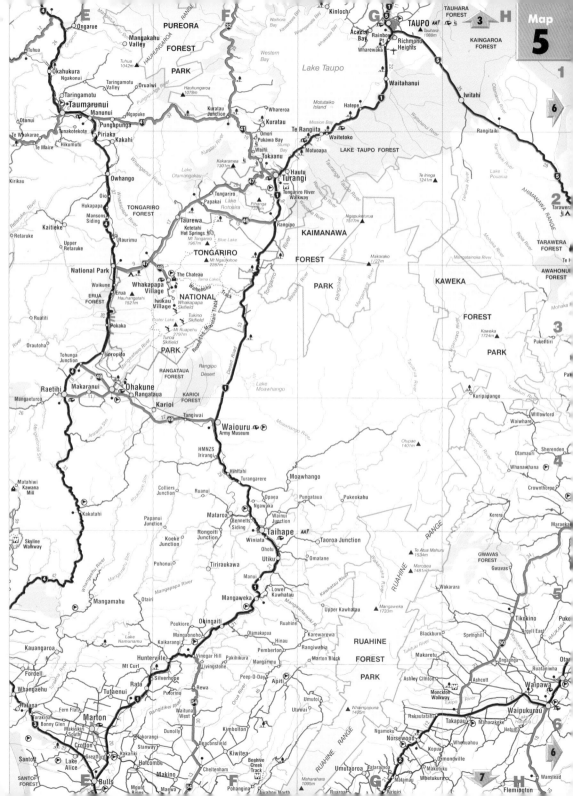

Map

5

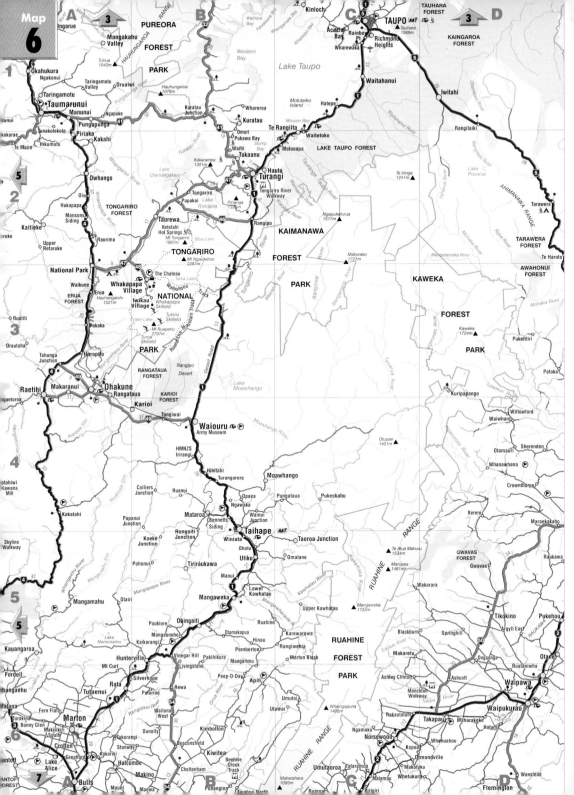

Map

6

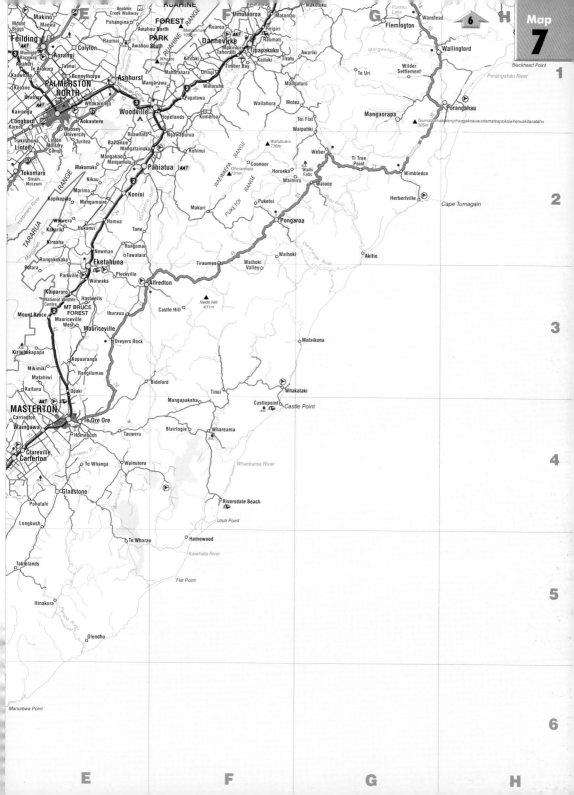

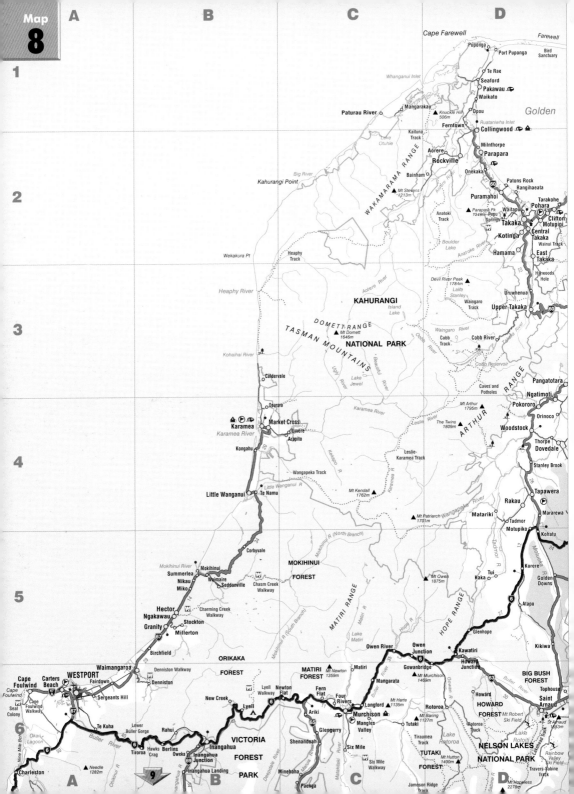

Map
8

	A	B	C	D

1

Cape Farewell
Farewell
Puponga
Port Puponga
Bird Sanctuary
Te Rae
Seaford
Pakawau
Waikato
Opou
Golden
Whanganui Inlet
Mangarakau
Knuckle Hill 506m
Paturau River
Kaituna Track
Ruataniwha Inlet
Ferntown
Collingwood
Milnthorpe
Parapara
Aorere
Bainham
Onekaka
Patons Rock
Rangihaeata
Rockville

2

WAKAMARAMA RANGE
Mt Stevens 1213m
Puramahoi
Parapara Pk 1249m
Pupu Springs
Waitapu
Takaka
Kotinga
Tarakohe
Pohara
Clifton
Motupipi
Central Takaka
Wainui Track
Harwoods Hole
Hamama
East Takaka
Kahurangi Point
Big River
Anatoki Track
Boulder Lake
Devil River Peak 1784m
Lake Stanley
Uruwhenua
Upper Takaka

3

Wekakura Pt
Heaphy Track
Heaphy River
Aotere River
KAHURANGI
Island Lake
Waingaro Track
Waingaro River
Cobb River
DOMETT RANGE
TASMAN MOUNTAINS
Mt Domett 1646m
NATIONAL PARK
Cobb Track.
Cobb River
Cobb Reservoir
Kohaihai River
Lake Jewel
Ugly River
Beautiful River
Pangatotara
ARTHUR RANGE
Ngatimoti
Caldervale
Caves and Potholes
Mt Arthur 1795m
Pokororo
Orinoco
Oparara
Woodstock
Leslie River
The Twins 1809m
Karamea
Market Cross
Umere
Arapito
Karamea River
Karamea River
Leslie-Karamea Track
Thorpe
Dovedale
Kongahu

4

Wangapeka Track
Stanley Brook
Tapawera
Little Wanganui R
Little Wanganui
Te Namu
Mt Kendall 1762m
Rakau
Mararewa
Mt Patriarch 1701m
Wangapeka River
Matariki
Tadmor
Motupiko
Kohatu
Corbyvale
Mokihinui R (North Branch)
Korere

5

Mokihinui River
Summerlea
Mokihinui
MOKIHINUI
FOREST
Tadmor River
Nikau
Waimaire
Seddonville
Chasm Creek Walkway
Miko
Mt Owen 1875m
Tui
Kaka
Golden Downs
Hector
Charming Creek Walkway
MATIRI RANGE
HOPE RANGE
Atapo
Ngakawau
Stockton
Mokihinui R (South Branch)
Granity
Millerton
Lake Matiri
Glenhope
Kikiwa
Birchfield
Owen River
Owen Junction
Kawatiri
Howard Junction

6

Cape Foulwind
Carters Beach
WESTPORT
Fairdown
Waimangaroa
Denniston Walkway
ORIKAKA
FOREST
MATIRI FOREST
Mt Newton 1359m
Matiri
Mangarata
Mt Murchison 1469m
Gowanbridge
Howard
BIG BUSH FOREST
Tophouse
Saint Arnaud
Cape Foulwind Walkway
Denniston
Lyell Walkway
Newton Flat
Fern Flat
Four Rivers
Mt Harte 7135m
HOWARD FOREST
Mt Robert Ski Field
Seal Colony
Sergeants Hill
New Creek
Lyell
Ariki
Murchison
Rotoroa
Howard
St Arnaud 1463m
Te Kuha
Lower Buller Gorge
Rahui
Mangles Valley
Tutaki
Mt Baring 1127m
Lake Rotoroa
Rotoroa Track
Rainbow Valley Ski Field
Okari Lagoon
Berlins
Glengarry
Shenandoah
Six Mile
Tiraumea Track
TUTAKI FOREST
NELSON LAKES NATIONAL PARK
Charleston
Tiroroa
Hawks Crag
Oweka
Inangahua Junction
VICTORIA FOREST PARK
Minehaha
Six Mile Walkway
Mt Hutton 1400m
Mt Hopeless 2278m
Travers-Sabine Track
Buller River
Inangahua
Inangahua Landing
Paenga
Jameson Ridge Track

9

Needle 1282m
Nine Mile Beach
Deepdale River

Map

8

E F G H

1

Spit

Bay

2

7

Cape Stephens

Stephens Is

Separation Point

Totaranui
Awaroa Bay

Moa Park
Totaranui Track

Marine Reserve
Tonga Is

**ABEL TASMAN
NATIONAL
PARK**
Mt Evans
1756m

Coast Track

Torrent Bay

Adele Is

Marahau

Kaiteriteri

Riwaka
Valley

Riwaka

Umukuri
Brooklyn

Motueka

Port Motueka

Motueka River

Tasman Bay

Lower
Moutere

Mariri
Jacket Is
Moutere Inlet

Braeburn

Kina
Tasman

Harakeke

Rosedale

Ruby Bay

Neudorf
Mahana
Mapua
Rabbit Is
Bronte
Tahunanui

Blackbird
Valley
Upper
Moutere

Port Nelson

NELSON

Redwoods
Valley

Bishopdale
Enner Glynn

Stoke

Dun Mountain
Walkway

Brightwater
Hope

Richmond

**GOLDEN
DOWNS
FOREST**
Wai-iti

Spring Grove

Wakefield

Foxhill

Belgrove

Hiwipango

D'Urville Is

Greville Harbour
Ragged Pt

Trio Is

D'Urville Pen

Chetwode Is

French Pass
(Anaru)

Paddock Rocks

Sauvage Pt

Bulwer

MARLBOROUGH SOUNDS

MARITIME PARK

Forsyth Is

Alligator Head
Cape Lambert
Cape
Jackson

Guards
Bay

Titirangi Bay

Port Gore

Cape Soucis

Croisilles
Harbour

Maud Is

Elaine Bay

Tawhitinui Reach

Beatrix
Bay

Anakoha
Bay

Endeavour
Inlet
Ship
Cove
Endeavour
Track

3

Whangamoa Head

Delaware
Bay

Pepin Is

Okiwi Bay

Tennyson
Inlet

Manaroa

Crail Bay

Motuara Is
Cape
Koami

Long Is

Glenduan
Cable Bay
Walkway
Wakapuaka
Hira

Marybank

Whangamoa

Carluke

Rai Valley

Nydia
Walkway

Nopera
Saint
Omer

Portage

Te Mahia

Waitaria
Bay

Anakiwa Track

Kenepuru
Head

Kenepuru
Track

Blumine

Queen

Arapa
Is

Pear
Hd

Tui Glen
Atawhai
Brooklands
Dodson Valley

Havelock

Moenui

Anakiwa

Charlotte Sound

Curious Cove

Cook
Strait

Pelorus Bridge

Canvastown

Linkwater

The
Grove

Waikawa

Picton

Mount Pleasant

Koromiko

Rununder Pt

BRYANT

RANGE

Pelorus

Rai

Robertson Pt

RICHMOND RANGE

Mt Royal
Track

Mt Richmond
1756m

Okaramio

Kaituna

Para

Rarangi

4

MOUNT RICHMOND

FOREST PARK

Onamalutu

Tuamarina

Marshlands

Spring Creek
Wairau Pa

Groveton

Wairau Bar

Wairau River

Cloudy Bay

5

7

Te Rou

Renwick
Fairhall

Woodbourne

BLENHEIM

Riverlands

Big Lagoon

Wither Hills
Walkway

White Bluffs

Lake Chalice
Track

Lake
Chalice

Wairau Valley

Wairau

Hillersden

Tyntesfield

Omaka Downs

Craiglochart
Summerlands

Avondale

Rossmore

Dashwood

Seddon

Blind River

Clifford Bay

Red Hill
1790m

The Branch

Netherwood

Altimarlock

Richmond
Brook

Marathon
Down

Lake Grassmere
Salt Works
L Grassmere

Hauwai

Cape
Campbell

Mt Phillips
1542m

Malvern
Hills

Welds Hill

Ward

6

**RAINBOW
FOREST**

Scotts Knob
2160m

Blue Mountain
2051m

Pudding Hill
1464m

Mt Munro
1481m

Gladstone

Jordan
Awapiri

Camden

Peggioh

Kilgram

Te Rapa

Mirza

Flaxbourne River

Wharanui

9

E F G H

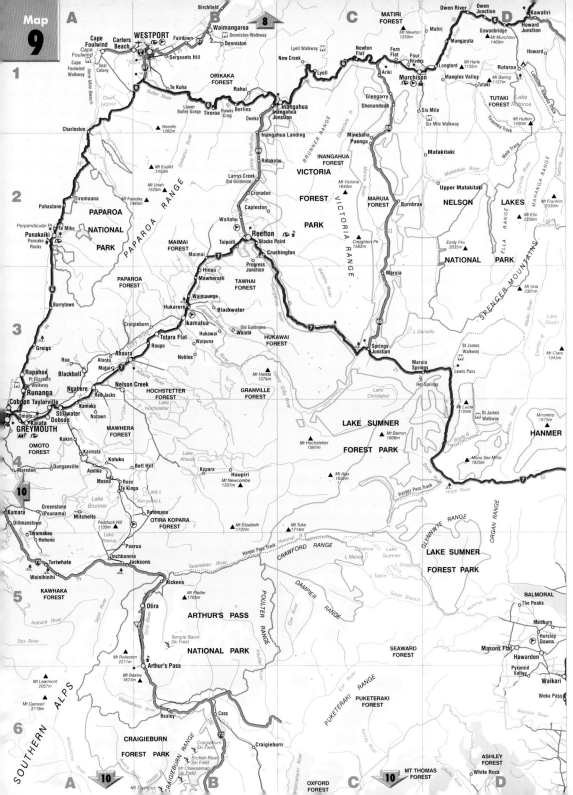

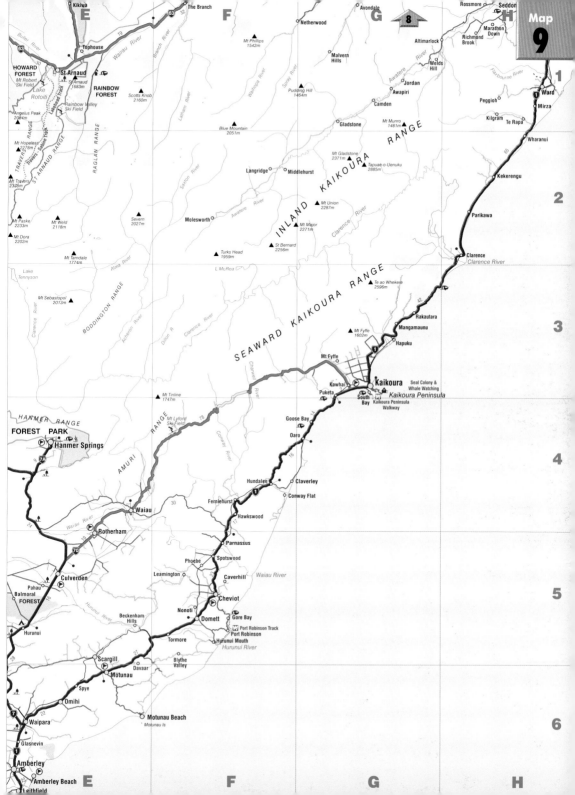

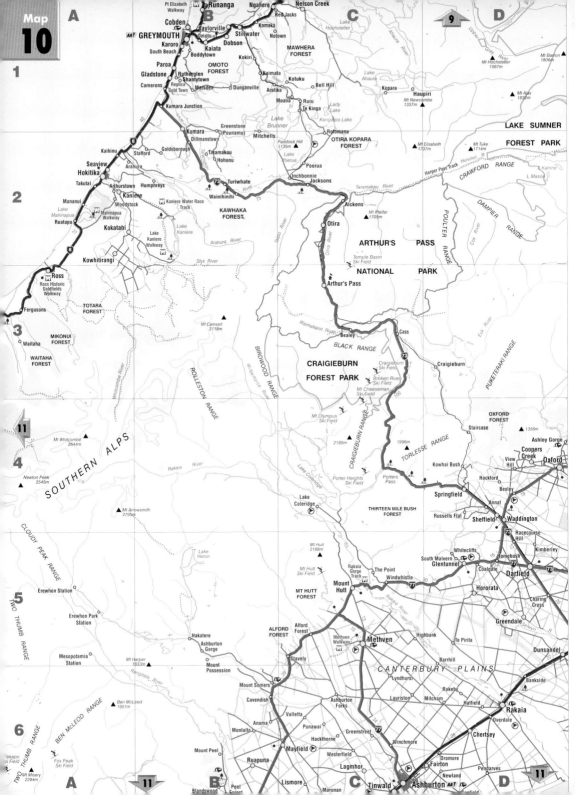

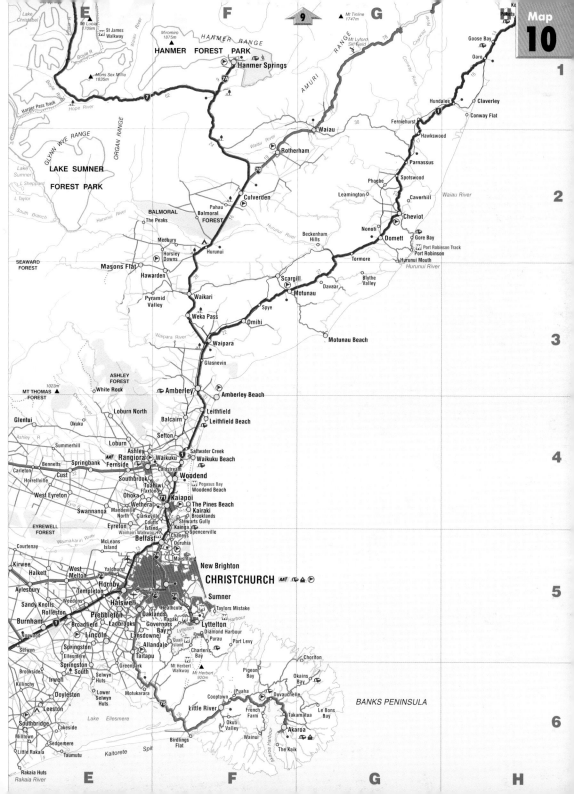

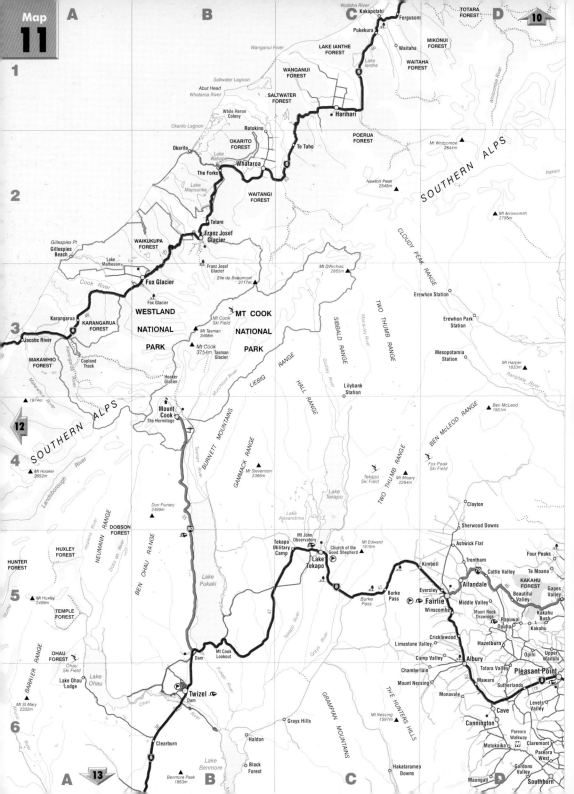

Map
12

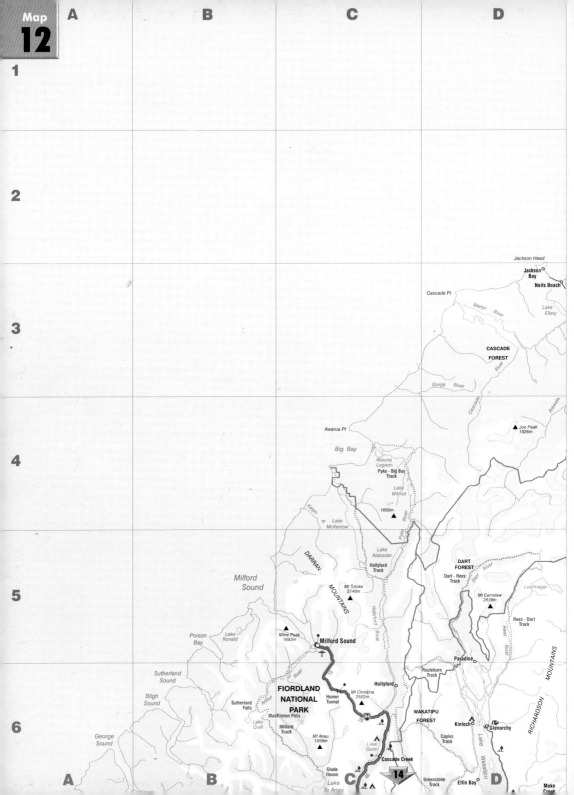

A **B** **C** **D**

1

2

3

Jackson Head

Jackson Bay

Neils Beach

Cascade Pt

Marlyr River

Lake Ellery

CASCADE

FOREST

Gorge River

Cascade River

Aawaroa

Awarua Pt

Joe Peak 1926m

Big Bay

Waiuna Lagoon

Pyke - Big Bay Track

4

Lake Wilmot

Kaipo R

1650m

Lake McKerrow

Pyke River

DARRAN

Lake Alabaster

DART FOREST

Dart - Rees Track

Dart River

Milford Sound

Hollyford Track

Lochnagar

Mt Tutoke 2746m

MOUNTAINS

Mt Earnslaw 2819m

5

Hollyford River

Rees - Dart Track

Poison Bay

Lake Ronald

Mitre Peak 1692m

Milford Sound

Rees River

RICHARDSON

Sutherland Sound

Paradise

Routeburn Track

Bligh Sound

Arthur River

FIORDLAND NATIONAL PARK

Hollyford

Mt Christina 2502m

Homer Tunnel

94

WAKATIPU FOREST

MOUNTAINS

Sutherland Falls

Kinloch

Glenorchy

Sutherland

MacKinnon Pass

Milford Track

Mt Anau 1958m

Caples Track

6

Lake Quill

Lake Gunn

Lake Wakatipu

George Sound

Glade House

Cascade Creek

14

Greenstone Track

Elfin Bay

Moke Creek

Lake Te Anau

A **B** **C** **D**

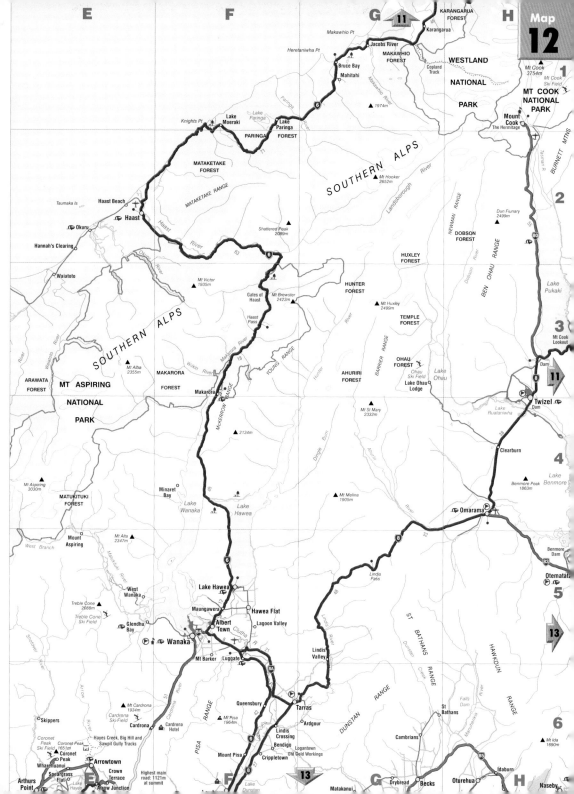

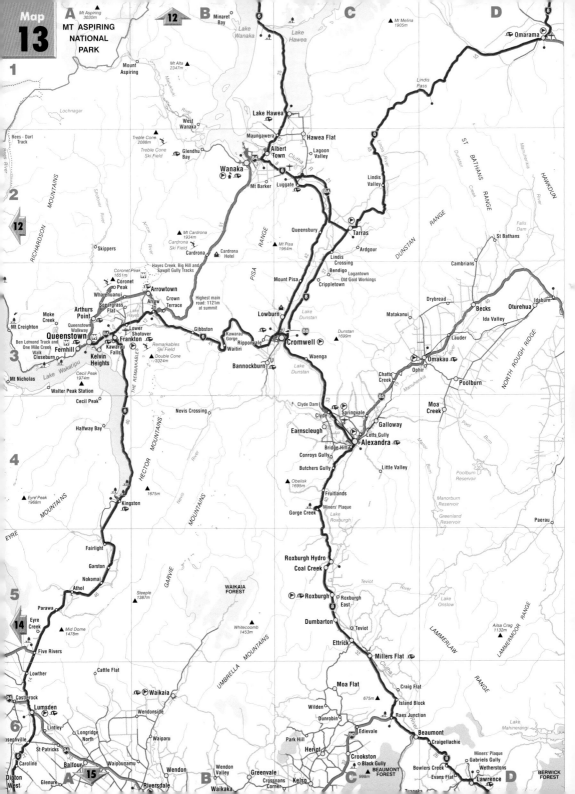

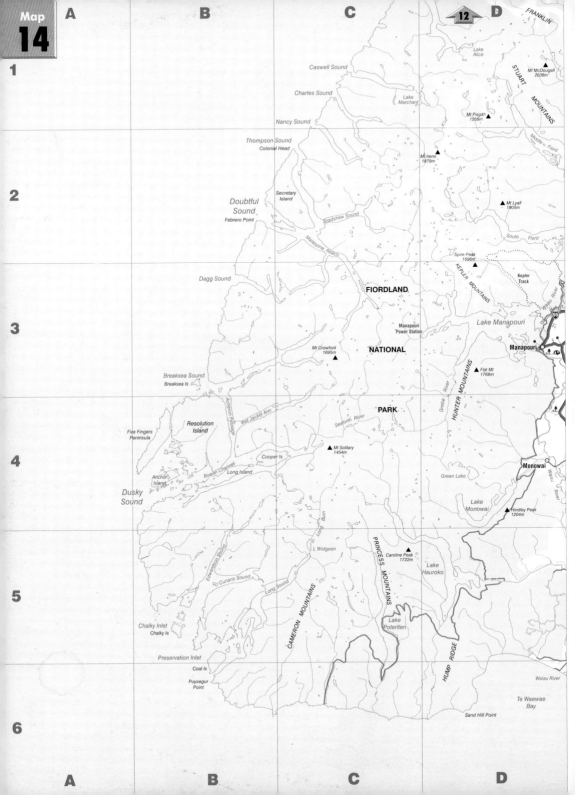

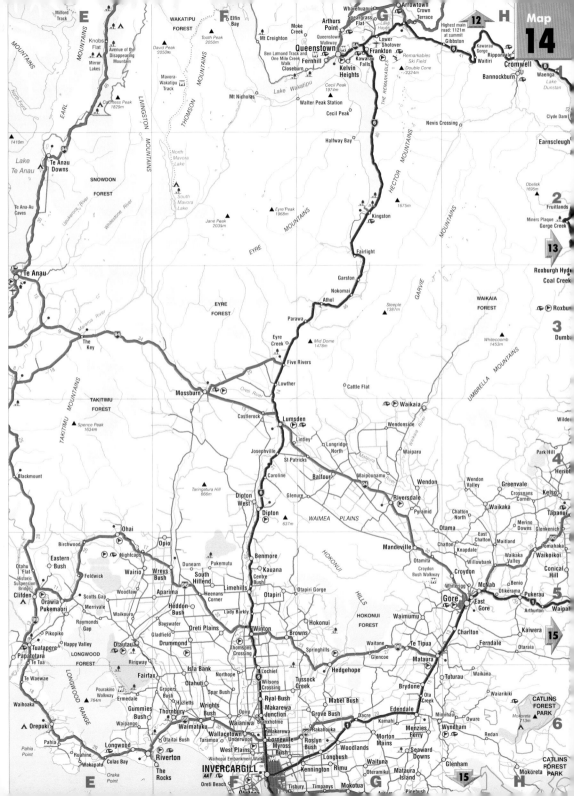

Map

14

Milford Track
E
WAKATIPU FOREST
F
Elfin Bay
Wharehuanui
Arrowtown
Crown Terrace
G
12
H
Highest main road: 1121m at summit Gibbston
8
Kawarau Gorge Ripponvale
Knobs Flat
Avenue of the Disappearing Mountain
Tooth Peak 2050m
Moke Creek
Speargrass Flat
Lake Hayes
Waitiri
Cromwell
Mt Creighton
Queenstown
Lower Shotover
Mirror Lakes
David Peak 2050m
Mt Nicholas
Ben Lomond Track and One Mile Creek Walk Closeburn
Fernhill
Queenstown Walkway
6A
Frankton
Kawarau Falls
Remarkables Ski Field
Double Cone ~2324m
Waenga
Lake Dunstan
Bannockburn
Cowless Peak 1829m
Kelvin Heights
Clyde Dam
Mavora-Wakatipu Track
Lake Wakatipu
Cecil Peak 1974m
Walter Peak Station
Nevis Crossing
Earnscleugh
1410m
Te Anau Downs
North Mavora Lake
Halfway Bay
THE REMARKABLES
40
HECTOR MOUNTAINS
1675m
Kingston
Obelisk 1695m
Fruitlands
Miners Plaque Gorge Creek
2
SNOWDON FOREST
South Mavora Lake
Eyre Peak 1968m
Te Ana-Au Caves
30
EYRE MOUNTAINS
Fairlight
GARVIE MOUNTAINS
13
Roxburgh Hyd Coal Creek
Te Anau
Garston
Nokomai
Steeple 1387m
WAIKAIA FOREST
Roxbu
Athol
Parawa
Dumba
9
The Key
94
34
EYRE FOREST
Eyre Creek
Mid Dome 1478m
Whitecoomb 1453m
UMBRELLA MOUNTAINS
3
Five Rivers
Lowther
20
TAKITIMU MOUNTAINS
TAKITIMU FOREST
Mossburn
Oreti River
Cattle Flat
Waikaia
Park Hill
Heriot
Spence Peak 1634m
Castlerock
Lumsden
Wendonside
Waiparu
Wendon Valley
Greenvale
Kelso
Lintley
Longridge North
Crossnans Corner
Merino Downs
Tapanui
Blackmount
Josephville
St Patricks
Balfour
Waipounamu
Riversdale
Chatton North
Waikaka
Glenkenich
Pomahaka
Waikoikoi
Caroline
Taringatura Hill 666m
Glenure
Pyramid
Otama
Chatton
East Chatton
Maitland
Willowbank
Waikaka Valley
Conical Hill
Ohai
Birchwood
Dipton West
Dipton
637m
WAIMEA PLAINS
Mandeville
Otamita
Croydon Bush Walkway
Knapdale
Benio
Otikerama
Pukerau
Waipai
5
Nightcaps
Opio
Benmore
HOKONUI HILLS
Croydon
Whiterigg
McNab
Arthurton
Eastern Bush
Wairio
Wreys Bush
Dunearn
Pukemutu
Kauana
Centre Bush
Otapiri Gorge
HOKONUI FOREST
Gore
East Gore
15
Feldwick
Woodlaw
South Hillend
Limehills
Otapiri
Waimumu
Charlton
Kaiwera
Otaraia
Otahu Flat
Historic Suspension Bridge
Scotts Gap
Aparima
Heenans Corner
Lady Barkly
Hokonui
Waitane
Te Tipua
Ferndale
Cliften
Orawia Pukemaori
Merrivale
Waikouro
Heddon Bush
Bayswater
Oreti Plains
Winton
Browns
Springhills
Glencoe
Mataura
Waiariki
Pikopiko
Raymonds Gap
Gladfield
Drummond
Thompsons Crossing
Waitane
Brydone
Tuturau
Waikana
Ota Creek
CATLINS FOREST PARK
6
Tuatapere
Papatotara
Te Tua
Happy Valley
LONGWOOD FOREST
Otautau
Ringway
Isla Bank
Northope
Tussock Creek
Hedgehope
Edendale
Mimihau
Oware
Mokoreta 713m
Te Waewae
Fairfax
Gropers Bush
Otahuti
Lochiel
Wilsons Crossing
Ryal Bush
Mabel Bush
Dacre
Kamahi
Menzies Ferry
Wyndham
Redan
LONGWOOD RANGE
Pourakino Walkway 764m
Hazletts
Spar Bush
Makarewa Junction
Grove Bush
Hakahoupa
Morton Mains
Seaward Downs
Waihoaka
Ermedale
Gummies Bush
Thornbury
Wrights Bush
Branxholme
Roslyn Bush
Waituna
Glenham
Orepuki
Waimatuku
Waianiwa
Lorneville
Myross Bush
Woodlands
Oteramika
Mataura Island
Mokoreta
Pahia Point
Waipango
Otaitai Bush
Wallacetown
Underwood
Taramoa
West Plains
Longbush
Rimu
CATLINS FOREST PARK
Pahia
Ruahine
Longwood
Waihopai Embankment Walk
INVERCARGILL
Kennington
Tisbury
Kapuka
Pukerau
Colac Bay
Riverton
The Rocks
Oreti Beach
Timpanys
Mokotua
Pinebush
15
Oraka Point
E
F
F
G
H

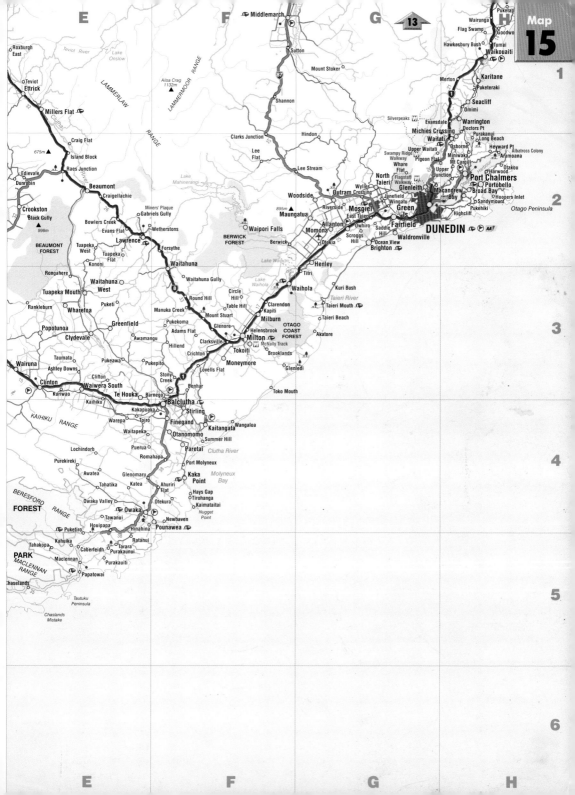

Index of New Zealand Place Names

The map number is listed in **bold** type, followed by the grid reference. Thus the name Acacia Bay can be found on **Map 3** (the map number is at the top outside corner of the page), and within the square indicated by grid numbers **E6**

Map number > 3/E6 < Grid reference

A

Acacia Bay 3E6
Adair................................11E6
Adams Flat................15F3
Ahaura 9A3
Ahikiwi.........................1D6
Ahikouka 7D4
Ahipara 1C4
Ahititi...........................5C1
Ahuriri Flat................15F4
Ahuroa 2D3
Aickens 9B5
Airedale 13G3
Aka Aka.....................3B1
Akaroa 10F6
Akatere 1D3
Akatore 15G3
Akerama....................1F5
Akitio........................7G2
Albany........................2D4
Albert Town 13B2
Albury........................11D5
Alexandra.................13C4
Alford Forest 10C5
Alfredton...................7E3
Alfriston 2E5
Algies Bay.................2D3
All Day Bay 13G6
Allandale 10F5
Allanton 13E6
Alma 13G3
Altimarlock Stn............9G1
Alton........................5C4
Amberley Beach..........9E6
Amberley...................9E6
Amodeo Bay...............2F4
Anakiwa...................8G4
Anakoha Bay.............8H3
Anama....................10B6
Anatimo....................8E2
Anawhata..................2C5
Aniwaniwa 6F1
Annat 10D4
Aokautere..................7E1
Aongatete....................3E2
Aorangi 4G3
Aorangi...................7E1
Aorere......................8D2
Aotea.........................3B4
Aotuhia....................5D3

Apanui.....................4D3
Apata..........................3E2
Apirama....................15B3
Apiti 5F6
Aponga......................1E6
Apotu.........................1F6
Aputerewa..................1D3
Arahiwi.......................3E4
Arahura 10A2
Aramatai 3C5
Aramiro 3B3
Aramoana...............13F6
Aramoana..................6E6
Aranga Beach...........1D6
Aranga 1D6
Arapae 3B5
Arapaoa 2C2
Araparera................2C3
Arapito 8C4
Arapohue 2B1
Arapuni 3D4
Ararata 5B4
Ararimu 2E6
Ararua 2C2
Aratapu 2B1
Aratika 9A4
Aratoro 3C5
Ardgour 13C2
Ardgowan 13G3
Ardkeen 6F2
Ardmore 2E5
Arero......................4G4
Argyll East...............5H5
Aria 3B6
Ariki........................8C6
Arno......................13G2
Arohena 3D4
Arowhenua Pa...........11E6
Arowhenua...............11E6
Arrow Junction 13B3
Arrowtown 13B3
Arthur's Pass............9B6
Arthurs Point 13A3
Arthurstown.............10A2
Arthurton 15D3
Arundel 11E4
Ashburton Forks 10C6
Ashburton Gorge 10B5
Ashburton 10C6
Ashcott 5H6
Ashers...................15C5

Ashhurst.....................7E1
Ashley Clinton.............5G6
Ashley Downs 15E3
Ashley Gorge 10D4
Ashley 10E4
Ashton 11F5
Ashwick Flat.............11D5
Atapo 8D5
Atarau 9A3
Atawhai 8F4
Athenree 3E1
Athol 13A5
Atiamuri 3E5
Auckland 2D5
Aukopae 5D2
Aurere 1D3
Auroa 5B4
Aviemore 13E1
Avoca 1E6
Avoca 9B6
Avondale 8F5
Awahou North 7E1
Awahou South............7E1
Awahou 3F4
Awahuri 7E1
Awaiti 3D1
Awakaponga 3G3
Awakeri Springs..........3G4
Awakeri 3G4
Awakino Point...........2B1
Awakino....................3A6
Awamangu 15E3
Awamarino 3B5
Awamoko 13G2
Awanui.....................1C3
Awanui.....................4F2
Awapiri Stn...............9G1
Awariki......................7G1
Awaroa Creek...........1F6
Awaroa....................13G3
Awaroa 1C4
Awarua 15B5
Awarua 1E5
Awatea 15E4
Awatere....................4H2
Awatoto 6E4
Awatuna 10B2
Awatuna 5B3
Awhitu Central...........2D6
Awhitu 2D6
Aylesbury 10E5

B

Back River...................1D3
Bainesse 7D2
Bainham....................8D2
Balcairn 10F4
Balclutha 15F3
Balfour....................13A6
Ballance 7E2
Balmoral...................9E5
Bankside 10D6
Bannockburn.............13B3
Barkes Corner............3E3
Barnego 15F3
Barrhill....................10D5
Barrytown...................9A3
Bartletts 6H2
Battersea 7D4
Bay View 6E4
Baylys Beach 2A1
Bayswater 15B3
Beachlands 2E5
Beaconsfield..............5F6
Bealey 9B6
Beaumont 13C6
Beautiful Valley 11D5
Beckenham Hills 9E5
Becks 13D3
Belfast 10F5
Belfield 11E6
Belgrove 8E4
Bell Block 5B2
Bell Hill 9A4
Bendigo...................13C3
Benhar.....................15F3
Benio......................15D3
Benmore 15B3
Bennetts Siding 5F4
Bennetts 10E4
Benneydale 3C6
Berlins 8B6
Berwick....................15F2
Bethlehem..................3E2
Bexley 10D4
Bideford.....................7E3
Big Bay 2D5
Big Omaha 2D3
Big River 9B3
Birchfield 8B5
Birchwood 15A3
Birdlings Flat 10F6
Bishopdale 8E4

Black Forest

Black Forest 11B6
Black Gully 13C6
Black Point 13F2
Blackball.....................9A3
Blackbird Valley 8E4
Blackburn...................5G5
Blackhead 7H1
Blackmount...............14D4
Blackpool 2E5
Blacks Point 9B2
Blackwater 9B3
Blairlogie...................7F4
Blandswood 11E4
Blenheim...................8G5
Blind River 8H5
Blue Cliffs 13G1
Bluff.......................15B5
Blythe Valley 9F5
Boddytown 10B1
Bombay 2E6
Bonny Glen 5E6
Bortons....................13F2
Bowentown 3E2
Bowlers Creek 13D6
Braeburn 8E3
Braigh 2C1
Branxholme...............15B4
Bridge Hill 13C4
Bridge Pa 6E5
Brighton 15G2
Brightwater................8E4
Brixton......................5B2
Broad Bay 13F6
Broad Gully 13G2
Broadfield................10E5
Broadlands 3F6
Broadwood 1D4
Bronte 8E4
Brookby.....................2E5
Brooklands 10F4
Brooklands 15F3
Brooklands 8E4
Brooklyn....................8E3
Brookside 10E6
Brown Owl 7C4
Browns Beach...........11E6
Browns 15B3
Bruce Bay 12G1
Brunswick 5D5
Bruntwood.................3C3
Brydone 15C4
Brynavon 1G6
Brynderwyn................2C2
Buckland 2E6
Buckland 3D3
Bulls 5E6

Bulwer.......................8G3
Bunnythorpe 7E1
Burke Pass...............11C5
Burnbrae 9C2
Burnham 10E5
Bushey 13F5
Butchers Gully 13C4

C

Caberfeidh 15E5
Cable Bay 1D3
Caldervale.................8B3
Cambrians 13D2
Cambridge 3D3
Camden Stn..............9G1
Camerons 10B1
Camp Valley 11D5
Cannington 11D6
Canvastown...............8F4
Cape Foulwind 8A6
Cape Reinga 1A1
Cappleston................9B2
Cardiff 5B3
Cardrona 13B2
Carew 11E4
Carleton 10E4
Carluke......................8F4
Carnarvon 7D1
Caroline....................13A6
Carrington 7E4
Carters Beach............8A6
Carterton 7E4
Cascade Creek 12C6
Cass..........................9B6
Castlecliff 5D5
Castlehill....................7F3
Castlepoint 7F4
Castlerock 15B2
Cattle Creek 13F1
Cattle Flat 13A6
Cattle Valley 11D5
Cave.........................11D6
Cavendish 10B6
Caverhill 9F5
Cecil Peak 13A4
Central Takaka 8D2
Centre Bush 15B3
Chamberlain 11D6
Chaneys 10F5
Charing Cross 10D5
Charleston.................8A6
Charlton 15D3
Charteris Bay 10F5
Chaslands 15E5
Chatto Creek............13C3
Chatton North 15D2

Chatton 15D3
Cheddar Valley............3H4
Cheltenham................5F6
Chertsey 10D6
Chesterfield..............10B1
Cheviot 9F5
Chorlton 10G5
Christchurch 10F5
Churchill....................3B1
Circle Hill 15F3
Clandeboye 11E5
Claremont 11D6
Clarence 9H2
Clarendon 15F3
Clareville 7E4
Claris.........................2F2
Clarkeville................10F4
Clarks Beach 2D6
Clarks Flat 15E2
Clarks Junction 13E6
Clarksville 15F3
Claverley 9F4
Clayton....................11D4
Clearburn 11B6
Clevedon 2E5
Clifden 15A3
Clifton 15B5
Clifton 15E3
Clifton 6F4
Clifton 8D2
Clinton......................15E3
Clive 6E4
Closeburn.................13A3
Cloustonville 7D4
Clyde........................13C4
Clydevale 15E3
Coal Creek...............13C5
Coalgate 10D5
Coatesville 2D4
Cobb River 8D3
Cobden 10B1
Colac Bay 15A4
Coldstream...............10F4
Coldstream...............11E5
Colliers Junction 5F4
Collingwood 8D2
Colville.......................2F4
Colyton 7E1
Conical Hill 15D3
Conroys Gully 13C4
Conway Flat 9F4
Cooks Beach 2G5
Coonoor 7F2
Coopers Beach 1D3
Coopers Creek..........10D4
Cooptown 10F6

Donnellys Crossing

Corbyvale...................8B5
Cornwallis 2D5
Coroglen 2G5
Coromandel................2F4
Coronet Peak 13A3
Corriedale.................13F3
Courtney 10E5
Coutts Island 10F5
Craig Flat 13C6
Craigellachie 13D6
Craigieburn 9B3
Craigieburn 9B6
Craiglochart................8F5
Crail Bay 8G3
Crichton....................15F3
Cricklewood 11D5
Crippletown..............13C3
Croften 5E6
Cromwell...................13C3
Cronadun 9B2
Crookston 13C6
Crossans Corner 15D2
Crown Terrace...........13B3
Crownthorpe 6D4
Croydon 15D3
Crushington................9B2
Culverden 9E5
Curious Cove 8H4
Cust.........................10E4
Cuthill.......................2D4

D

Dacre 15C4
Dairy Flat 2D4
Dalefield....................7D4
Dannevirke 7F1
Darfield 10D5
Dargaville 2B1
Dashwood..................8H5
Davaar.......................9E5
Dawson Falls..............5B3
Deborah....................13G3
Deep Creek 13G2
Denniston..................8B6
Diamond Harbour.......10F5
Diggers Valley 1C4
Dillmanstown............10B2
Dipton West..............15B2
Dipton......................15B2
Dobson......................9A4
Doctors Point...........13F6
Dodson Valley 8F4
Dome Valley...............2D3
Domett......................9F5
Donnellys Crossing......1D6

Douglas

Douglas	13G2	Ermedale	15A4
Douglas	5C3	Erua	5E3
Dovedale	8D4	Esk Valley	13G1
Doyleston	10E6	Eskdale	6E4
Dreyers Rock	7E3	Ethelton	9E5
Dromore	10D6	Ettrick	13C5
Drummond	15B3	Eureka	3C3
Drury	2E6	Evans Flat	13D6
Drybread	13D3	Evansdale	13F6
Dumbarton	13C5	Eversley	11D5
Dunback	13F4	Eyre Creek	13A5
Dunearn	15B3	Eyreton	10E4
Dunedin	13F6		
Dunganville	9A4	**F**	
Dunmore	3B2	Fairburn	1D3
Dunollie	9A3	Fairdown	8A6
Dunolly	5F6	Fairfax	15B4
Dunrobin	13C6	Fairfield	13F6
Dunsandel	10D5	Fairhall	8G5
Duntroon	13F2	Fairlie	11D5
Duvauchelle	10F6	Fairlight	13A5
Dyerville	7D5	Fairton	10D6
		Fairview	11E6
E		Featherston	7D4
Ealing	11E5	Feilding	7E1
Earnscleugh	13C4	Feldwick	15A3
East Chatton	15D3	Fencourt	3D3
East Coast Bays	2D4	Fergusons	10A3
East Egmont	5B3	Fern Flat	1D4
East Gore	15D3	Fern Flat	5E6
East Taieri	13E6	Fern Flat	8C6
East Takaka	8D2	Ferndale	15D3
Eastbourne	7C5	Fernhill	13A3
Eastern Bush	15A3	Fernhill	6E4
Edendale	15C4	Ferniehurst	9F4
Edgecumbe	3G4	Fernside	10E4
Edievale	13C6	Ferntown	8D1
Egmont Village	5B2	Finegand	15F4
Eiffelton	11F5	Five Rivers	13F3
Eight Mile Junction	3C5	Five Rivers	13A5
Eketahuna	7E3	Flag Swamp	13F5
Elaine Bay	8G3	Flaxmere	6E4
Elderslie	13G3	Flaxton	10F4
Elephant Hill	13G2	Flemington	11F5
Elfin Bay	14F1	Flemington	5H6
Elgin	11F4	Fordell	5E6
Ellesmere	10E5	Forsyth	15F2
Elsthorpe	6E6	Fortification	15D5
Elstow	3D2	Fortrose	15C5
Eltham	5B3	Four Peaks	11D5
Endeavour Inlet	8H3	Four Rivers	8C6
Enfield	13G3	Fox Glacier	11B3
Enner Glynn	8E4	Foxhill	8E4
Epworth	11E5	Foxton Beach	7D2
Erewhon Park Stn	10A5	Foxton	7D2
Erewhon Station	10A5	Frankton	13A3

Franz Josef Glacier	11B2	**Hakatere**	
Frasertown	6G2	Glorit	2C3
French Farm	10F6	Golden Cross	3D1
French Pass	3D3	Golden Downs	8D5
French Pass	8G2	Golden Springs	3F5
Fruitlands	13C4	Golden Valley	3E1
Fuchsia Creek	13F3	Goldsborough	10B2
		Goodwood	13F5
G		Goose Bay	9F4
Gabriels Gully	13D6	Gordon	3E2
Galatea	3G5	Gordons Valley	11D6
Galloway	13C4	Gordonton	3C2
Gapes Valley	11D5	Gore Bay	9F5
Garston	13A5	Gore	15D3
Georgetown	13G2	Gorge Creek	13C4
Geraldine Downs	11E5	Gorge Road	15C5
Geraldine Flat	11E5	Governors Bay	10F5
Geraldine	11E5	Gowanbridge	8D6
Gibbston	13B3	Grahams Beach	2D6
Gillespies Beach	11A2	Granity	8B5
Gimmerburn	13E3	Grays Corner	13G2
Gisborne Point	3F4	Grays Hills	11C6
Gisborne	4F6	Greatford	5E6
Gladfield	15B3	Green Island	13F6
Gladstone Stn	9G1	Green Valley	13F4
Gladstone	10B1	Greendale	10D5
Gladstone	7D3	Greenfield	15E3
Gladstone	7E4	Greenhills	15B5
Glasnevin	9E6	Greenhithe	2D4
Glen Afton	3B2	Greenpark	10E6
Glen Massey	3B2	Greenpoint	15B5
Glen Murray	3B1	Greenstone	9A4
Glen Oroua	7D1	Greenstreet	10C6
Glenavy	13G2	Greenvale	13B6
Glenbervie	1F6	Greigs	9A3
Glenbrook Beach	2D6	Greta	9E5
Glenbrook	2D6	Greymouth	10B1
Glencoe	15C3	Greytown	7D4
Glendhu Bay	13B2	Gropers Bush	15B4
Glendhu	7E5	Grove Bush	15C4
Glenduan	8F3	Grovetown	8G5
Glengarry	8C6	Gummies Bush	15A4
Glenham	15D4	Gumtown	1F6
Glenhope	8D5	Guthrie	3E5
Gleniti	11E6	Gwavas	5H5
Glenkenich	15D3		
Glenledi	15F3	**H**	
Glenleith	13F6	Haast Beach	12E2
Glenomaru	15E4	Haast	12E2
Glenorchy	12D6	Hackthorne	10C6
Glenore	15F3	Hadlow	11E6
Glenpark	13F4	Hahei	2G5
Glentui	10E4	Hairini	3C4
Glentunnel	10D5	Hakaru	2D2
Glenure	15B2	Hakataramea Downs	11C6
Glinks Gully	2B2	Hakataramea	13F2
		Hakatere	10B5

Hakatere

Hakatere....................11F5
Haku.............................3B5
Halcombe...................5E6
Haldane 15D5
Haldon......................11B6
Halfmoon Bay 15B6
Halfway Bay 13A4
Halkett......................10E5
Halswell....................10E5
Hamama 8D2
Hamilton.....................3C3
Hampden 13G4
Hamua 7E2
Hamurana 3F4
Hangaroa 4E6
Hangaroa....................6G1
Hangatiki....................3C5
Hanmer Springs..........9E4
Hannahs Bay..............3F4
Hannahs Clearing 12E2
Happy Valley 15A3
Happy Valley 2E6
Hapuku 9G3
Harakeke....................8E4
Harapepe....................3C3
Harihari....................11C1
Hariki Beach..............4F2
Harrisville 2E6
Haruru 1E4
Harwood....................13F6
Hastings 6E5
Hastwells...................7E3
Hatepe 5G1
Hatfield....................10D6
Hatfields Beach..........2D4
Hatuma 5H6
Hauiti 4G5
Haumoana 6E4
Hauparu Bay 3F4
Haupiri.......................9B4
Hautanoa 4G4
Hautapu 3C3
Hautu.........................5F2
Hauturu 3B4
Hauwai.......................8H6
Havelock North 6E5
Havelock 8G4
Hawai 4E3
Hawarden 9D5
Hawea Flat...............13C2
Hawera.......................5B4
Hawkesbury Bush 13F5
Hawkswood 9F4
Hays Gap 15F4
Haywards 7C4
Hazelburn 11D5

Hazletts 15B4
Heathcote 10F5
Heatherlea 7D2
Hector 8B5
Heddon Bush 15B3
Hedgehope 15C4
Heenans Corner 15B3
Helena Bay..................1F5
Helensbrook 15F3
Helensville 2C4
Helvetia 2D6
Henderson 2D5
Henley 15G2
Hepburn Creek 2D3
Herbert 13F4
Herbertville 7G2
Herekino 1C4
Heriot 13C6
Hexton 4F6
Heywood Point 13F6
Hicks Bay 4G2
Highbank...................10C5
Highcliff 13F6
Hihi.............................1D3
Hihitahi 5F4
Hikuai........................2G6
Hikumutu....................5E2
Hikurangi 1F5
Hikutaia......................3D1
Hikuwai 4G4
Hilderthorpe..............13G3
Hillend 15F3
Hillersden 8F5
Hillgrove 13G4
Hillsborough 5B2
Hilton 11E5
Himatangi Beach 7D1
Himatangi...................7D2
Hinahina 15E4
Hinakura.....................7E5
Hinau..........................5F5
Hinau..........................9B3
Hindon......................13E6
Hinds 11F5
Hinehopu 3F4
Hinuera 3D3
Hira.............................8F4
Hiruharama................4G3
Hiwipango 8E5
HMNZS Irirangi 5F4
Hoanga.......................2B1
Hobsonville 2D5
Hodderville 3D4
Hoe-O-Tainui..............3C2
Hohonu 9A5
Hokio Beach 7D2

Hokitika 10A2
Hokonui....................15C3
Holdens Bay 3F4
Hollyford...................12C6
Homebush 10D5
Homebush 7E4
Homewood 7F5
Honikiwi......................3B4
Hook Bush 13G1
Hook 13G2
Hoopers Inlet............13F6
Hope 8E4
Hopelands 7F1
Hopeone 3H5
Horahora....................1G6
Horahora....................3D4
Horeke 1D4
Hornby 10E5
Horoeka 7F2
Horoera 4H2
Horohoro 3E5
Horopito 5E3
Hororata 10D5
Horotiu 3C2
Horrellville 10E4
Horsham Downs 3C2
Horsley Downs............9D5
Hospital Hill 4D3
Hot Water Beach 2G5
Hoteo North 2C3
Houhora 1C2
Houipapa...................15E4
Houpoto 4E3
Houto 1E6
Howard Junction 8D5
Howard 8D6
Howick 2E5
Huanui........................4F5
Huapai 2D4
Huarau 2C2
Huia............................2D5
Huiakama....................5C3
Huiarua.......................4G4
Huinga 5C3
Huirangi......................5B2
Huiroa 5C3
Hukanui......................7E2
Hukapapa....................5E2
Hukarere 9B3
Hukatere 2C2
Hukawai 9B3
Hukerenui...................1F5
Humphreys................10B2
Hundalee....................9F4
Hungahunga 3D2
Hunter 13G1

Hunterville 5F5
Huntingdon...............11F4
Huntly.........................3C2
Hunua 2E6
Hupara 1E5
Hurford 5B2
Hurleyville 5C4
Hurunui Mouth............9F5
Hurunui 9E5
Hyde..........................13E4

I

Ida Valley 13D3
Idaburn.....................13D3
Ihakara 7D2
Ihungia 4G4
Ihuraua 7E3
Ikamatua 9B3
Ikawai 13G2
Inaha 5B4
Inangahua Junction......8B6
Inangahua Landing 8B6
Inangahua...................8B6
Inch Valley 13F4
Inchbonnie 9A5
Incholme 13F3
Inglewood...................5B2
Invercargill...............15B4
Irwell........................10E6
Isla Bank 15B4
Island Block 13C6
Island Block 3C1
Island Cliff 13F2
Island Stream 13F3
Island View.................3E1
Ivydale 1D5
Iwikau Village 5F3
Iwitahi........................5H1

J

Jackson Bay 12D3
Jacksons 9A5
Jacobs River 11A3
Janefield...................13F6
Jerusalem 5D4
Johnsonville 7B5
Jordan.........................8G6
Josephville 15B2
Judgeford 7C4

K

Kaeo............................1E3
Kaharoa.......................3F4
Kahika 6E3
Kahoe 1D3
Kahuika 15E5

Kahuika

Kahutara

Kahutara 7D5
Kai Iwi Beach 5D5
Kai Iwi 5D5
Kaiaka 1D4
Kaiapoi 10F4
Kaiata 9A4
Kaiaua 2F6
Kaihere 3C1
Kaihiku 15E4
Kaihinu 10A2
Kaihu 1D6
Kaikarangi 5F5
Kaikohe 1E5
Kaikou 1E5
Kaikoura 9G3
Kaimamaku 1F5
Kaimarama 2G5
Kaimata 5B2
Kaimata 9A4
Kaimataitai 15F4
Kaimaumau 1C3
Kaimiro 5B3
Kainga 10F4
Kaingaroa Forest 3G5
Kaingaroa 1C3
Kainui 3C2
Kaipaki 3C3
Kaipara Flats 2D3
Kaiparoro 7E3
Kaipikari 5C2
Kairakau Beach..........6E6
Kairaki 10F4
Kairanga 7E1
Kairangi 3D4
Kairara 1E6
Kairua 3F2
Kaitaia 1C4
Kaitangata 15F4
Kaitaratahi 4F5
Kaitawa 6F1
Kaitemako 3F3
Kaiteriteri 8E3
Kaitieke 5E2
Kaitoke 5D6
Kaitoke 7F1
Kaituna 7E3
Kaituna 8G5
Kaiwaka 2C2
Kaiwera 15D3
Kaiwhaiki 5D5
Kaka Point 15F4
Kaka 8D5
Kakahi 5E2
Kakahu Bush 11D5
Kakahu.....................11D5
Kakanui....................13G3

Kakanui 2C3
Kakapotahi...............11C1
Kakapuaka 15F4
Kakaramea 5C5
Kakariki 4H3
Kakariki 5E6
KakariKI 7E2
Kakatahi 5E4
Kamahi.....................15C4
Kamaka 9A4
Kamo 1F6
Kanakanaia 4F5
Kaniere 10A2
Kaniwhaniwha............3B3
Kanohi.......................2D4
Kapiro 1E4
Kapiti 15F3
Kaponga 5B3
Kapowairua 1B1
Kapuka South 15C5
Kapuka.....................15C5
Kapuni 5B4
Kara...........................1F6
Karahaki.....................5C4
Karaka 2E6
Karakariki 3C3
Karamea 8B4
Karamu 3C3
Karangahake 3D1
Karangarua 11A3
Karapiro 3D3
Karatia 1B1
Karehana Bay 7C4
Karekare 2C5
Kareponia 1C3
Karere 7E1
Karetu.......................1F5
Karewarewa 5G5
Karioi 5F4
Kariotahi...................2D6
Karitane 13F5
Karori 7B5
Karoro 10B1
Karuhiruhi 1D5
Katea........................15E4
Katikati 3E2
Katiki 13G4
Katui.........................1D6
Kauana.....................15B3
Kauangaroa 5E5
Kauearanga 2G6
Kaukapakapa............2C4
Kaupokonui 5B4
Kauri Flat 3B3
Kauri.........................1F6
Kauroa 3B3

Kauru Hill..................13F3
Kauwhata 7E1
Kawa 2F2
Kawakawa Bay...........2E5
Kawakawa 1E5
Kawarau Falls............13A3
Kawatiri 8D5
Kawerau 3G4
Kawerua 1D6
Kawhia 3B4
Kawiti 1E5
Kekerengu..................9H2
Kelchers 13G2
Kellys Bay 2B2
Kelso 15D2
Kelvin Heights 13A3
Kenana 1D3
Kenepuru Head..........8H3
Kennedy Bay 2F4
Kennington 15C4
Kereone 3D2
Kerepehi 3D1
Kereru 5H4
Kererutahi 3H4
Kereta 2F5
Keretu 4E5
Kerikeri Inlet 1E4
Kerikeri 1E4
Kerrytown 11E6
Kia Ora 13G3
Kihikihi 3C4
Kihitu.........................6G2
Kikiwa 8D5
Kilgram 9H1
Killinchy 10E6
Kimbell 11D5
Kimberley 10D5
Kimbolton 5F6
Kimihia 3C2
Kina...........................8E3
Kingsdown 11E6
Kingseat 2D6
Kingston 13A4
Kinleith 3E5
Kinloch 12D6
Kinloch 3E6
Kinohaku....................3B4
Kiokio 3C4
Kirikau 5E2
Kirikopuni 1E6
Kiripaka 1F6
Kiritaki 7F1
Kiritehere 3A5
Kiriwhakapapa 7E3
Kirwee 10E5
Kiwi 8D5

Kiwitahi 3D3
Kiwitea.......................5F6
Knapdale 15D3
Koeke Junction 5F5
Kohatu 8D5
Kohe 1C4
Kohekohe...................2D6
Kohi 5C5
Kohika 13G1
Kohinui 7F2
Kohukohu 1D4
Kohumaru 1D3
Kohuratahi.................5D2
Koitiata 5D6
Kokako 6F1
Kokatahi 10A2
Kokiri 9A4
Kokoamo 13F2
Kokonga 13E4
Komakorau..................3C2
Komata North.............3D1
Komata 3D1
Komokoriki 2D3
Kongahu......................8B4
Konini 15E2
Konini 7E2
Kopaki 3C5
Kopane 7E1
Kopara.......................9B4
Kopikopiko..................7E2
Kopu 2F6
Kopua 5H6
Kopuarahi...................2F6
Kopuaranga 7E3
Kopuaroa 4G3
Kopuawhara 6H2
Kopuku 2E6
Kopuriki 3G5
Koputaroa 7D2
Korakonui 3C4
Koranga 4E5
Koremoa 2B2
Korere 8D5
Korito 5B2
Koromatua 3C3
Koromiko....................8G4
Koru 5A2
Kotare 5C1
Kotemaori 6F2
Kotinga 8D2
Kotuku 9A4
Kourawhero................2D3
Koutu 1D5
Kowhai Bush 10D4
Kowhai 9G3
Kowhatu 13F1

Kowhatu

Kowhitirangi

Mangatara

Kowhitirangi 10A2
Kuaotunu 2G4
Kukumoa....................4D3
Kumara Junction 10B1
Kumara 10B1
Kumeroa....................7F1
Kumeu 2D4
Kupe...........................5B3
Kuratau Junction 5F1
Kuratau........................5F1
Kuri Bush 15G3
Kuriheka 13F3
Kuripapango 5H3
Kuriwao 15E3
Kurow 13F2
Kutarere....................3H4
Kyeburn Diggings.......13E3
Kyeburn.....................13E3

L

Ladbrooks 10E5
Lady Barkly 15B3
Lagmhor....................10C6
Lagoon Valley 13C2
Laingholm 2D5
Lake Alice 5E6
Lake Coleridge............10C4
Lake Ferry...................7D5
Lake Grassmere 8H6
Lake Hawea 13C1
Lake Hayes 13B3
Lake Moeraki.............12F1
Lake Ohau Lodge 11A6
Lake Ohia 1C3
Lake Okareka.............3F4
Lake Okareka.............3F4
Lake Paringa 12F1
Lake Tekapo..............11C5
Lake Waitaki..............13E2
Lakeside....................10E6
Langridge 9F2
Langs Beach...............2D2
Lansdowne................10E5
Larrys Creek 9B2
Lauder.......................13D3
Lauriston 10C6
Lawrence 15E2
Le Bons Bay 10G6
Leamington 3C3
Leamington 9F5
Lee Flat....................13E6
Lee Stream 13E6
Lees Valley................9C6
Leeston 10E6
Leigh 2D3
Leithfield Beach..........10F4

Leithfield.....................10F4
Lepperton...................5B2
Letts Gully.................13C4
Levels Valley 11D6
Levels........................11E6
Levin 7D2
Lichfield.....................3D4
Lilybank Stn 11C3
Limehills 15B3
Limestone Downs 3B1
Limestone Valley........11D5
Lincoln......................10E5
Lindis Crossing 13C2
Lindis Valley 13C2
Linkwater 8G4
Lintley.......................13A6
Linton Military Camp 7E2
Linton 7E2
Lismore 10C6
Little Bay 2F4
Little Huia....................2D5
Little Rakaia 10E6
Little River 10F6
Little Valley 13C4
Little Waihi 3F3
Little Wanganui 8B4
Livingstone 13F3
Livingstone 5F5
Loburn North 10E4
Loburn 10E4
Loch Norrie 2C4
Lochiel......................15B4
Lochindorb 15E4
Long Bay 2D4
Long Beach 13F6
Longbeach 11F5
Longburn....................7E1
Longbush 15C4
Longbush 7E4
Longford......................8C6
Longlands 6E5
Longridge North 13A6
Longwood 15A4
Lorneville...................15B4
Lovells Flat 15F3
Lowburn....................13C3
Lowcliffe....................11F5
Lower Hutt 7C5
Lower Kaimai 3E3
Lower Kawhatau..........5F5
Lower Moutere 8E3
Lower Selwyn Huts 10E6
Lower Shotover 13A3
Lower Waihou 1C5
Lowther 13A6
Luggate 13C2

Lumsden 13A6
Lyalldale 13G1
Lyell...........................8B6
Lyndhurst 10C6
Lynmore 3F4
Lyttelton...................10F5

M

Maata 5B3
Mabel Bush 15C4
Macandrew Bay..........13F6
Mackaytown 3D1
Maclennan 15E5
Macraes Flat 13F4
Maeraweka................13F3
Maerewhenua 13F2
Maewa 7E1
Mahana 8E4
Mahanga 6H2
Maharahara 7F1
Maharakeke 5H6
Maheno......................13G3
Mahia Beach 6H2
Mahia.........................6H2
Mahinepua 1E3
Mahitahi....................12G1
Mahoe 5B3
Mahoenui 3B6
Mahora........................4H3
Mahurangi West..........2D3
Mahurangi...................2D3
Mahuta 2B1
Mahuta 3C2
Maihiihi......................3C4
Maimai 9B2
Maioro Sands..............3B1
Maioro 3A1
Mairoa........................3B5
Maitland 15D3
Makahu.......................5C3
Makakaho Junction 5D4
Makakaho 5D4
Makara Beach..............7B5
Makara 7B5
Makaraka 4F6
Makaranui 5E3
Makarau 2C4
Makaretu 5G5
Makarewa Junction 15B4
Makarewa 15B4
Makarora 12F3
Makauri 4F6
Makerua 7D2
Maketu Pa 3B4
Maketu 3F3
Makikihi....................13G1

Makino........................5F6
Makirikiri South 5E6
Makirikiri.....................7F1
Makomako..................3B3
Makomako..................7E2
Makorori.....................4G6
Makotuku 5G6
Makuri 7F2
Malvern Hills...............8F6
Mamaku......................3E4
Mamaranui 1E6
Manaia 5B4
Manakau.....................7D3
Mananui 10A2
Manapouri 14D3
Manaroa 8G3
Manawahe 3G4
Manawaora..................1F4
Manawaru 3D2
Mandeville North 10E4
Mandeville 15C3
Mangaeturoa 5E4
Mangahao 7E2
Mangaiti.....................3D2
Mangakahu Valley........5E1
Mangakino 3D5
Mangakura 2C3
Mangakuri Beach 6E6
Mangamahu 5E5
Mangamaire 7E2
Mangamaunu 9G3
Mangamingi.................5C3
Mangamuka Bridge......1D4
Mangamuka 1D4
Mangamutu 7E2
Mangaonoho 5F5
Mangaorapa 7G1
Mangaore....................7D2
Mangaorongo...............3C4
Mangaotaki 3B5
Mangapa......................1D4
Mangapai.....................1F6
Mangapakeha 7F4
Mangaparo...................5D1
Mangapehi 3C6
Mangapiko Valley 3C1
Mangapiko 3C3
Mangarakau 8C1
Mangarata 8C6
Mangarawa..................7F1
Mangarimu 5F5
Mangaroa.....................7D4
Mangatainoka..............7F2
Mangataiore 1D4
Mangatangi 2E6
Mangatara....................2B1

Mangataraire

Mangataraire...............1D5
Mangatarata.................3C1
Mangatawhiri................2E6
Mangatea....................3C5
Mangateparu................3D2
Mangateretere.............6E4
Mangatoetoe................1D4
Mangatoi....................3F3
Mangatoki...................5B3
Mangatoro...................7F1
Mangatu.....................1D6
Mangatuna.................4G5
Mangatutu..................3C4
Mangawara.................3C2
Mangaweka.................5F5
Mangawhai Heads.......2D2
Mangawhai.................2D2
Mangawhata.............7D2
Mangawhero.............1D5
Mangere....................2D5
Mangles Valley............8C6
Mangonui..................1D3
Mangorei...................5B2
Mangungu..................1D4
Maniatutu.................3F3
Manly.......................2D4
Manoeka...................3F3
Mansons Siding..........5E2
Manui......................5F5
Manuka Creek...........15F3
Manukau City.............2D5
Manukau..................1C4
Manunui...................5E1
Manurewa.................2D5
Manutahi..................5B4
Manutuke..................4F6
Mapau.....................2B2
Mapiu......................3C6
Mapua.....................8E4
Maraehara................4H2
Maraekakaho............6D4
Maraeroa..................1D4
Maraetaha................6H1
Maraetai..................2E5
Maraetai..................3D5
Marahau...................8E3
Maramarua Mill..........2E6
Maramarua...............2F6
Mararewa.................8D4
Marathon Down Stn.....9H1
Maratoto..................3D1
Mareretu..................2C2
Marima....................7E2
Mariri......................8E3
Market Cross.............8B4
Marlow....................1F5

Marohemo.................2C2
Marokopa.................3A5
Maromaku................1E5
Maronan..................11E4
Maropiu...................1D6
Marsden Bay.............1F6
Marsden Point...........2D1
Marsden..................10B1
Marshland...............10F5
Marshlands..............8G5
Martinborough..........7D5
Marton Block.............5G5
Marton....................5E6
Marua.....................1F5
Maruia Springs..........9C3
Maruia.....................9C3
Marumaru.................6G2
Marybank.................5D6
Marybank.................8F4
Masons Flat.............9D5
Massey University.......7E2
Massey....................2D5
Masterton.................7E4
Mata.......................1D4
Mata.......................2C1
Matahanea................4D4
Matahapa.................3H4
Matahi.....................3H5
Matahina..................3G4
Matahiwi..................5E4
Matahiwi..................7E3
Matahuru.................3C1
Matai.......................3D3
Matai.......................9A3
Mataikona................7G3
Matakana.................2D3
Matakanui...............13C3
Matakawau...............2D6
Matakohe.................2C2
Matamata.................3D3
Matamau..................5G6
Matangi...................3C3
Matangirau..............1E3
Matapihi...................3F2
Matapouri................1G5
Matapu....................5B4
Matarangi................2G4
Matarau...................1F6
Mataraua..................1E5
Matarawa................7D4
Matariki...................8D4
Mataroa...................5F4
Matata.....................3G3
Matatoki..................2G6
Matau......................5C2
Mataura Island.........15C4

Mataura..................15C3
Matauri Bay..............1E3
Matawai...................4E5
Matawaia.................1E5
Matawhero...............4F6
Matemateaonga..........5C3
Matiere....................5D1
Matihetihe................1C5
Matingarahi..............2F5
Matira.....................3B2
Matiri......................8C6
Mauku.....................2D6
Maungakaramea..........1F6
Maungapohatu...........3H6
Maungatapere............1F6
Maungatapu..............3F2
Maungatautari...........3D3
Maungati..................11D6
Maungatiro...............13F1
Maungatua...............13E6
Maungaturoto............2C2
Maungawera.............13C2
Maunu.....................1F6
Mauriceville West.......7E3
Mauriceville...............7E3
Mawaro...................11D6
Mawheraiti................9B3
Maxwell...................5D5
Mayfield..................10C6
Maymorn..................7D4
Mayton...................13G2
McLeans Island.........10E5
McLeod Bay..............1G6
McNab...................15D3
Meadowbank...........13F5
Medbury..................9D5
Meeanee..................6E4
Menzies Ferry..........15C4
Mercer....................2E6
Meremere.................3C1
Meremere.................5C4
Merino Downs..........15D2
Merita.....................1D2
Merrijigs..................9B3
Merrivale................15A3
Merton...................13F5
Mesopotamia Stn......10A5
Methven..................10C5
Michies Crossing.......13F6
Middle Valley...........11D5
Middlehurst...............9F2
Middlemarch...........13E5
Midhirst...................5B3
Mihi........................3F6
Mihiwaka................13F6
Mikimiki...................7E3

Miko........................8B5
Milford Sound...........12C5
Milford....................11E5
Mill Creek.................2G5
Millburn...................15F3
Millers Flat..............13C5
Millerton...................8B5
Milltown..................10E6
Milnthorpe...............8D2
Milton....................15F3
Mimihau.................15D4
Mimiwhangata Bay.......1F5
Mina.......................9F5
Minaret Bay............12F4
Minden....................3E3
Minehaha.................8C6
Minginui...................3G6
Miranda...................2F6
Mirza......................8H6
Mitcham.................10D6
Mitchells..................9A4
Mitimiti....................1C5
Mititai.....................2B1
Moa Creek..............13D4
Moa Flat.................13C6
Moana.....................9A4
Moawhango.............5F4
Moeatoa...................3A5
Moeawatea...............5C4
Moehau...................1D5
Moengawahine...........1E6
Moenui....................8G4
Moeraki..................13G4
Moerangi..................3B3
Moerewa..................1E5
Moeroa....................5C3
Moewhare................2C1
Mohaka...................6F2
Mokai......................3E6
Mokara....................6E3
Mokau.....................1F5
Mokau.....................3A6
Mokauiti...................3C6
Moke Creek.............13A3
Mokihinui.................8B5
Mokoia....................5B4
Mokoreta................15D4
Mokotua.................15C4
Molesworth Stn.........9F2
Momona.................13E6
Monavale...............11D6
Monavale.................3C3
Moneymore.............15F3
Monowai................14D4
Montalto................10B6
Moonlight...............13E4

Moonlight

Morere   **Omaka Downs**

Morere 6H2	Murchison 8C6	Ngataki.......................1B2	Ohakune 5E3
Morrinsville................3D2	Muriwai Beach 2C5	Ngatamahine...............3B6	Ohangai 5B4
Morrisons Bush...........7D4	Muriwai.......................4F6	Ngatapa......................4F6	Ohapi 11E5
Morrisons 13F4	Muriwai.......................6H1	Ngatea 3D1	Ohau............................7D5
Morton Mains 15C4	Murupara 3G5	Ngatimoti....................8D4	Ohaua.........................3H6
Morven......................13G2	Myross Bush 15B4	Ngatira 3E4	Ohauiti.........................3E3
Mosgiel.....................13E6		Ngawaka 5F4	Ohaupo.......................3C3
Mossburn 15B2	**N**	Ngawapurua 7F2	Ohautira 3B3
Motairehe 2F2	Naenae 7C5	Ngawha Springs.........1E5	Ohawe 5B4
Motatau 1E5	Naike 3B2	Ngawha.......................1E5	Ohineakai 4G3
Motea.........................7G1	Naperape 9F5	Ngawihi 7D6	Ohinepaka...................6F2
Moteo.........................6E4	Napier 6E4	Ngongotaha Valley 3E4	Ohinepanea.................3G3
Motu...........................4E4	Naseby.......................13E3	Ngongotaha.................3F4	Ohinewai 3C2
Motueka 8E3	National Park 5E3	Ngunguru....................1G6	Ohingaiti 5F5
Motukaika 11D6	Naumai.......................2B2	Ngutunui 3C4	Ohoka 10E4
Motukaraka 1D5	Neils Beach...............12D3	Ngutuwera 5C5	Ohope 3H4
Motukarara................10E6	Nelson Creek 9A3	Niagara 15D5	Ohotu 5F5
Motukiore 1D5	Nelson.........................8E4	Nightcaps 14E5	Ohura 5D1
Motumaoho.................3D2	Nenthorn 13E5	Nihoniho 5D1	Ohuri 1D5
Motunau Beach............9E6	Netherton 3D1	Nikau 7E2	Oio 5E2
Motunau 9E6	Netherwood.................8F5	Nikau 8B5	Okaeria 3C1
Motunui 5B2	Neudorf 8E4	Nireaha 7E2	Okahu 1C4
Motuoapa...................5G2	Nevis Crossing 13B4	Nobles.........................9B3	Okahu 2B1
Motupiko 8D4	New Brighton...............10F5	Nokomai 13A5	Okahukura 5E1
Motupipi 8D2	New Creek 8B6	Nonoti.........................9F5	Okaihau.......................1E4
Motutangi 1C3	New Plymouth.............5B2	Nopera 8G3	Okains Bay 10G6
Motuti 1D5	Newbury......................7E1	Normanby 11E6	Okaiwa 5B4
Motutoa......................1D5	Newhaven 15F4	Normanby 5B4	Okaka 1D4
Moumahaki 5C5	Newland....................10D6	Norsewood 5G6	Okaramio 8G4
Mount Aspiring...........12E5	Newman......................7E2	North Egmont..............5B3	Okarito 11B2
Mount Barker 13B2	Newstead 3C3	North River...................2C1	Okato 5A2
Mount Bruce...............7E3	Newton Flat 8C6	North Taieri................13F6	Okau 5C1
Mount Cargill 13F6	Ngaere 5B3	Northope 15B4	Okauia Pa 3E3
Mount Cook 11B4	Ngahape 3C4	Norton Reserve 13G2	Okauia.........................3E3
Mount Hutt 10C5	Ngahere 9A3	Norwood....................10E5	Okere Falls 3F4
Mount Maunganui 3F2	Ngahinapouri 3C3	Notown........................9A4	Okete 3B3
Mount Peel 10B6	Ngaiotonga 1F4	Nuhaka 6H2	Okiato 1F4
Mount Pisa................13C3	Ngakawau 8B5	Nukuhou North 3H4	Okiore 4D4
Mount Pleasant...........8G4	Ngakonui 5E1	Nukumaru 5D5	Okitu 4G6
Mount Possession......10B5	Ngakuru 3E5	Nukuroa 13G2	Okiwi Bay 8F3
Mount Somers...........10B6	Ngamatapouri 5D4	Nukutawhiti 1E6	Okiwi 2F2
Mount Stoker.............13E5	Ngamoku.....................5G6		Okoia 5D5
Mount Stuart 15F3	Ngapaenga 3B5	**O**	Okoki...........................5C2
Mount Wesley 2B1	Ngapara 13F3	aklands......................10E5	Okoroire 3D3
Mourea 3F4	Ngapeke 3F3	Oakleigh 1F6	Okuku........................10E4
Moutoa 7D2	Ngapipito 1E5	Oakura 1F5	Okupu.........................2F3
Moutohora...................4E4	Ngapuhi......................1E5	Oakura 5A2	Okura 2D4
Mt Aspiring................13B1	Ngapuke 5E1	Oamaru 13G3	Okuru 12E2
Mt Biggs 7E1	Ngapuna 13E5	Oaonui 5A3	Okuti Valley 10F6
Mt Creighton 13A3	Ngaputahi 3G6	Oaro............................9G4	Omaha Flats 2D3
Mt Fyffe......................9G3	Ngararatunua 1F6	Ocean Beach.............1G6	Omaha 2D3
Mt Nessing................11D6	Ngarimu Bay 2F6	Ocean Beach 6F5	Omahu.........................2G6
Mt Nicholas 13A3	Ngaroma 3D5	Ocean View 15G2	Omahu.........................6E4
Muhunoa East............7D3	Ngaroto 3C4	Oeo 5A4	Omahuta 1D4
Muhunoa 7D2	Ngarua........................3D2	Ohaeawai 1E4	Omaio..........................4F3
Mukahanga.................8G2	Ngaruawahia 3C2	Ohai 15A3	Omaka Downs 8G5

Omakau

Omakau	13D3	Opononi	1C5
Omakere	6E6	Oporo	15B4
Omamari	2A1	Opotiki	4E3
Omana	2B1	Opou	8D1
Omanaia	1D5	Opouriao	3H4
Omanawa	3E3	Opoutama	6H2
Omanu Beach	3F2	Opouteke	1E6
Omanu	3F2	Opoutere	2G6
Omapere	1C5	Opua	1F4
Omarama	13D1	Opuatia	3B1
Omarumutu	4E3	Opuawhanga	1F5
Omata	5A2	Opuha	11D5
Omatane	5G5	Opunake	5A4
Omaunu	1D4	Oraka Beach	6H2
Omiha	2E5	Orakau	3C4
Omihi	9E6	Orakeikorako	3E5
Omimi	13F5	Orakipaoa	11E6
Omoana	5C3	Orangimea	5D4
Omokoroa Beach	3E2	Oraora	1D5
Omokoroa	3E2	Orapiu	2E5
Omori	5F1	Orari Bridge	11E5
Omoto	10B1	Orari	11E5
Onaero	5B2	Orautoha	5E3
Onamalutu	8G5	Orawau	1D4
One Tree Point	1F6	Orawia	15A3
Onekaka	8D2	Orepuki	15A4
Onemana	2G6	Orere Point	2F5
Onepoto	6F1	Orere	2F5
Onepu	3G4	Oreti Beach	15B4
Onerahi	1F6	Oreti Plains	15B3
Oneriri	2C3	Orewa	2D4
Oneroa	2E4	Oringi	7F1
Onetangi	2E5	Orini	3C2
Onewhero	3B1	Orinoco	8D4
Ongaonga	5H5	Ormond	4F6
Ongarue	3C6	Ormondville	5G6
Ongaruru	4G4	Oromahoe	1E4
Onoke	1D5	Orongo Bay	1F4
Opaea	5F4	Orongo	2F6
Opaheke	2E6	Oropi	3E3
Opahi	1E5	Orton	11E5
Opaki	7E3	Orua Bay	2D5
Opaku	5C4	Orua Downs	7D1
Opapa	6E5	Oruaiti Beach	4F2
Opape	4E3	Oruaiti	1D3
Opara	1D5	Oruaiwi	5E1
Oparara	8B4	Oruanui	3E6
Oparau	3B4	Oruawharo	2C2
Oparure	3B5	Oruru	1D3
Opatu	5D2	Osborne	13F6
Ophir	13D3	Ostend	2E5
Opihi	11D5	Ota Creek	15C4
Opiki	7D2	Otaha	1E4
Opio	15B3	Otahei Bay	1F4
Opito	2G4	Otahu Flat	14E5
Oponae	4D4	Otahuti	15B4

Otaika Valley	1F6	Otway	3D2
Otaika	1F6	Oue	1D5
Otaio Gorge	13G1	Oueroa	6E6
Otaio	13G1	Ouruhia	10F5
Otairi	5E5	Outram	13E6
Otaitai Bush	15B4	Overdale	10D6
Otakairangi	1F6	Owaka Valley	15E4
Otakeho	5B4	Owaka	15F4
Otaki Beach	7C3	Oware	15D4
Otaki Forks	7D3	Oweka	8B6
Otaki	7D3	Owen Junction	8C5
Otakiri	3G4	Owen River	8C5
Otakou	13F6	Owhango	5E2
Otama	15C3	Owhata	1C4
Otamakapua	5F5	Owhata	3F4
Otamaroa	4F2	Owhiro	13E6
Otamauri	5H4	Owhiwa	1F6
Otamita	15C3	Oxford	10D4
Otane	3H5		
Otane	6D5	**P**	
Otangaroa	1D4	Paekakariki	7C4
Otangiwai	3B6	Paenga	9C2
Otanomomo	15F4	Paengaroa	3F3
Otao	1E4	Paepaerahi	3D4
Otapiri Gorge	15B3	Paerata Ridge	3H4
Otapiri	15B3	Paerata	2E6
Otara	15D5	Paerau	13D4
Otara	4E3	Paeroa	3D1
Otaraia	15D3	Paewhenua	3C5
Otaramarae	3F4	Pahau	9E5
Otatara	15B4	Pahautane	9A2
Otaua	1D5	Pahi	2C2
Otaua	3B1	Pahia	15A4
Otautau	15A3	Pahiatua	7E2
Otehirinaki	4E3	Pahoia	3E2
Otekaieke	13F2	Pahou	3H4
Otekura	15F4	Paiaka	1F5
Otematata	13E1	Paihia	1E4
Oteramika	15C4	Pakanae	1D5
Otewa	3C4	Pakaraka	1E4
Otiake	13F2	Pakawau	8D1
Otikerama	15D3	Pakeho	3B5
Otipua	11E6	Pakihikura	5F5
Otira	9B5	Pakipaki	6E5
Otiria	1E5	Pakiri	2D2
Otokia	15G2	Pakotai	1E6
Otoko	4E5	Pakowhai	6E4
Otonga	1F5	Palm Beach	2E4
Otoroa	1E3	Palmerston North	7E1
Otorohanga	3C4	Palmerston	13F5
Otuhi	1F6	Pamapuria	1C4
Otunui	5E1	Panetapu	3D4
Oturehua	13D3	Pangatotara	8D3
Oturoa	3E4	Panguru	1C5
Oturu	1C3	Papaaroha	2F4
Otuwhare	4F3	Papakai	5F2

Papakai

Papakaio | | | **Puketotara**

Papakaio	13G3	Pataua	1G6

Papakaio 13G3
Papakura 2E6
Papamoa Beach..........3F3
Papamoa 3F3
Papanui Junction 5F4
Paparangi 5D5
Paparata......................2E6
Paparimu.....................2E6
Paparoa 2C2
Paparore 1C3
Papatawa 7F1
Papatea 4F2
Papatoetoe 2D5
Papatotara.................14E5
Papatowai 15E5
Papawai 7D4
Papawera 4G3
Paponga 1D4
Papua 1D5
Papueru 3G6
Para 8G4
Paradise...................12D5
Parahi.........................2B2
Parakai 2C4
Parakao.......................1E6
Paranui........................1D3
Paraoanui Pa 3H5
Parapara 1D3
Parapara 8D2
Paraparaumu Beach 7C3
Paraparaumu 7C4
Parau 2D5
Parawa 13A5
Parawai 2F6
Parawera 3C4
Parekarangi 3F5
Parekura Bay...............1F4
Paremata 4G5
Paremoremo 2D4
Pareora West 11D6
Pareora 13G1
Paretai 15F4
Parewanui 7D1
Parikawa 9H2
Parikino 5E5
Pariokara 4F3
Park Hill 13C6
Parkhurst 2C4
Parkville 7E3
Parnassus 9F5
Paroa Bay...................1F4
Paroa 10B1
Paroa 3H4
Parore 2B1
Parua Bay 1G6
Patangata...................6E6

Pataua 1G6
Patea 5C5
Patearoa 13E4
Paterangi.....................3C3
Patetonga 3D1
Patoka........................6D3
Patons Rock...............8D2
Patumahoe 2D6
Paturau River 8C1
Patutahi 4F6
Paua 1B1
Pauanui.......................2G5
Pauatahanui 7C4
Pawarenga 1C4
Peebles 13G3
Peel Forest................11E4
Peep-O-Day 5F6
Peggioh Stn 9H1
Pehiri 4E6
Pekapekarau 1E6
Pekerau 1C3
Pelorus Bridge............8F4
Pemberton..................5F5
Pembroke 5B3
Pendarves 10D6
Pentland Hills 13F2
Pepepe 3B2
Peria 1D3
Peria 3D3
Petone........................7C5
Phoebe.......................9F5
Piarere 3D3
Picton.........................8G4
Pigeon Bay 10F6
Pigeon Flat 13F6
Piha............................2C5
Pihama.......................5A4
Pikes Point...............13G2
Pikiwahine..................2C1
Pikopiko 15A3
Pikowai 3G3
Pine Bush 15C5
Pinedale 3D4
Piopio 3B5
Pios Beach.................3E2
Pipiriki 5D4
Piproa 2F6
Pipiwai 1E6
Piriaka 5E2
Pirinoa 7D5
Piripai 3H3
Piripaua 6F1
Piripiri 3B4
Piripiri 7F1
Pirongia 3C4
Piropiro 3C6

Pleasant Point...........11D6
Pleasant Valley..........11E5
Pleckville 7E3
Plimmerton 7C4
Poerua 9A5
Pohangina 7E1
Pohara........................8D2
Pohatukura 4G3
Pohonui 5F5
Pohuehue....................2D3
Pohukura 5C2
Point Wells 2D3
Pokaka 5E3
Pokapu 1E5
Pokeno 2E6
Pokororo 8D4
Pokuru 3C4
Pollock 2D6
Pomahaka 15D3
Pomerangai 3B5
Ponatahi 7E4
Ponga 2E6
Pongakawa Valley 3F3
Pongakawa 3F3
Pongaroa 7F2
Poolburn 13D3
Popotunoa 15E3
Porangahau 7H1
Porirua East 7C4
Porirua 7C4
Porootarao 3C6
Poroporo 3H4
Poroti 1F6
Poroutawhao 7D2
Port Albert...................2C3
Port Chalmers 13F6
Port Charles 2F4
Port Fitzroy 2F2
Port Jackson...............2F3
Port Levy...................10F5
Port Molyneux 15F4
Port Motueka 8E3
Port Nelson 8E4
Port Ohope 3H4
Port Puponga..............8D1
Port Robinson 9F5
Port Waikato................3B1
Portage.......................8G4
Portland 1F6
Portobello 13F6
Potaka.........................4G2
Pouawa 4G6
Poukawa 6E5
Poukiore 5F5
Pounawea 15F4
Pourere 6E6

Pouto...........................2C3
Prebbleton................10E5
Progress Junction 9B2
Progress Valley 15D5
Puaha........................10F6
Puahue 3C4
Puakauiti 15E5
Puerua 15E4
Puha...........................4F5
Puhata 1C4
Puhipuhi 1F5
Puhoi..........................2D3
Pukahu.......................6E5
Pukapuka 2D3
Pukawa Bay 5F2
Pukearuhe 5C1
Pukeatua.....................3D4
Pukeawa 15E3
Pukehiki....................13F6
Pukehina 3F3
Pukehou......................6D5
Pukehuia 2B1
Pukekapia 3C2
Pukekaroro 2C2
Pukekawa 3B1
Pukekohe East............2E6
Pukekohe....................2E6
Pukekoma 15F3
Pukekura...................11C1
Pukekura.....................3D3
Pukemaori 15A3
Pukemiro 3B2
Pukemoremore 3D3
Pukemutu 15B3
Pukengahu..................5C3
Pukenui.......................1C2
Pukeokahu...................5G4
Pukeoware 2D6
Pukepito 15E3
Pukepoto....................1C4
Pukerau 15D3
Pukerimu 3C3
Pukeroro 3C3
Pukerua Bay 7C4
Puketa 9G3
Puketaha.....................3C2
Puketapu 13F5
Puketapu.....................6E4
Puketeraki 13F5
Puketi 15E3
Puketi 1E4
Puketiro.....................15E4
Puketitiri 5H3
Puketoi 7F2
Puketona.....................1E4
Puketotara 3C4

Puketurua

Puketurua 3D4
Puketutu.....................3C5
Pukeuri 13G3
Punakaiki 9A2
Punakitere Valley..........1F5
Punakitere..................1D5
Punaruku....................1F5
Punawai 10C6
Punehu 1C5
Pungaere 1E4
Pungapunga................5E1
Pungarehu 5A3
Pungarehu 5E5
Pungataua 5G4
Puni.........................2D6
Puniho 5A2
Puniwhakau 5C3
Puponga 8D1
Pupuke 1D4
Purakanui 13F6
Purakaunui...............15E5
Puramahoi 8D2
Purangi 2G5
Purangi 5C2
Purekireki 15E4
Pureora 3D6
Purerua 1E4
Puriri 2G6
Purua 1F6
Pururu 3C5
Putara 7E3
Putaruru 3D4
Putorino....................5F6
Putorino....................6F3
Puwera 1F6
Pyes Pa 3E3
Pyramid Valley 9D6
Pyramid....................15C2

Q

Quarry Hills 15D5
Queens Flat..............13F3
Queensbury 13C2
Queenstown.............13A3

R

Racecourse Hill.........10D5
Raes Junction 13C6
Raetihi 5E3
Raglan......................3B3
Rahotu 5A3
Rahui.........................8B6
Rai Valley 8F4
Rainbow Point 3E6
Raio 1C2
Rakahouka................15C4

Rakaia Huts 10E6
Rakaia.....................10D6
Rakau.......................8D4
Rakaumanga 3C2
Rakaunui...................3B4
Rakauroa 4E5
Rakautao...................1E5
Rakautara 9G3
Rakautatahi 5G6
Ramanui...................5D3
Ramarama 2E6
Ranana 5D4
Ranfurly...................13E3
Rangataua 5E3
Rangatira Valley 11E5
Rangi Point 1C5
Rangiahua 1D4
Rangiahua 6F2
Rangiaowhia 3C4
Rangiatea 3C4
Rangihaeata 8D2
Rangiora 10E4
Rangiotu 7D2
Rangipo 5F2
Rangipu.....................3B3
Rangiputa 1C3
Rangiriri West 3C1
Rangiriri 3C1
Rangitaiki 5H1
Rangitata Island 11E5
Rangitata..................11E5
Rangitihi 1C4
Rangitoto 3C5
Rangitukia 4H3
Rangitumau................7E3
Rangiuru....................3F3
Rangiwahia................5G5
Rankleburn...............15E3
Ranui 2D5
Rapahoe 9A3
Rapaki 10F5
Rapanui....................5D5
Rapaura....................8G5
Rapuwai 11D5
Rarangi 8G4
Rata 5E6
Ratana 5E6
Ratanui...................15E5
Ratapiko 5B3
Raukawa 6D5
Raukokore 4F2
Raumai......................7E1
Raumati Beach 7C4
Raumati South 7C4
Raumati.....................7F1
Raupo 2B2

Raupo 9B3
Raupunga...................6F2
Raurimu 5E2
Rawene.....................1D5
Rawhia 1D4
Rawhiti 1F4
Rawhitiroa 5B3
Raymonds Gap 15A3
Red Beach 2D4
Red Hill 2E6
Red Jacks 9A3
Redan 15D4
Redhill 2B2
Redruth 11E6
Redvale 2D4
Redwoods Valley.........8E4
Reefton 9B2
Reena 1C5
Rehia 2B2
Rehutai.....................2A1
Reidston 13G3
Reikorangi 7C3
Remuera Settlement 1E5
Renown.....................3B2
Renwick....................8G5
Reotahi Bay 1G6
Repia 2B2
Reporoa 3F5
Reporua 4H3
Rere 4E5
Rerewhakaaitu 3F5
Retaruke 5E2
Rewa 5F6
Rewanui 9A3
Rewarewa 3C5
Rewiti.......................2C4
Richmond Brook Stn....9H1
Richmond Downs........3D3
Richmond Heights 5G1
Richmond 13G3
Richmond 8E4
Rimu 15C4
Ringway 15A4
Riponui 1F5
Ripponvale 13B3
Rissington 6E4
Riverhead 2D4
Riverlands..................8G5
Riverlea 5B3
Riversdale Beach 7F4
Riversdale 15C2
Riverside 11F5
Riverside 13E6
Riverton...................15A4
Riwaka Valley 8E3
Riwaka 8E3

Ruaroa

Roa 9A3
Rock and Pillar..........13E4
Rockford..................10D4
Rockville 8D2
Rokeby....................10D6
Rolleston 10E5
Romahapa.................15F4
Rongahere 15E3
Rongoiti Junction..........5F5
Rongokokako 7E2
Rongomai...................7E2
Rongotea 7D1
Roseberry 13G3
Rosedale 8E4
Rosewill...................11E6
Roslyn Bush.............15C4
Ross 10A3
Rossmore Stn 9H1
Rotherham 9E5
Rotoehu.....................3F4
Rotoiti 3F4
Rotokakahi.................1C4
Rotokauri 3C3
Rotokautuku 4G3
Rotokawa 3E6
Rotokawa 3F4
Rotokino 11B1
Rotokohu....................9B2
Rotomahana................3F5
Rotomanu 9B4
Rotongaro 3B2
Rotongata 3D4
Rotoorangi 3D3
Rotoroa 8D6
Rotorua 3F4
Rototuna 2B2
Rototuna 3C2
Rotowaro 3B2
Round Hill 15F3
Rowan 5B3
Roxburgh East 13C5
Roxburgh Hydro.........13C5
Roxburgh 13C5
Ruahine....................15A4
Ruahine 5F5
Ruakaka.....................2C1
Ruakituri....................4E6
Ruakokoputuna 7D5
Ruamahanga 2F5
Ruanui 5F4
Ruapekapeka 1F5
Ruapuke.....................3B3
Ruapuna 10B6
Ruarangi 2C1
Ruaroa 1C4
Ruaroa 7F1

Ruatahuna

Ruatahuna 3H6
Ruatangata West..........1F6
Ruataniwha.................5H6
Ruatapu 10A2
Ruatiti........................5E3
Ruato.........................3F4
Ruatoki North..............3H4
Ruatoria.....................4G3
Ruawai.......................2B2
Ruawaro.....................3B2
Ruawhata...................7E2
Ruby Bay....................8E4
Rukuhia......................3C3
Rukuwai......................1G6
Runanga 9A3
Runaruna....................1C4
Runciman...................2E6
Ruru 9A4
Russell 1F4
Russells Flat 10D4
Rutherglen 10B1
Ryal Bush..................15B4

S
Saddle Hill 13F6
Saies.........................1D3
Salisbury 11E6
Saltwater Creek..........10F4
Sandspit.....................2D3
Sandy Knolls 10E5
Sandymount 13F6
Sanson.......................7D1
Santoft.......................5E6
Scarborough 11E6
Scargill 9E5
Scotsman Valley 3D3
Scotts Gap 15A3
Scroggs Hill 15G2
Seacliff.....................13F5
Seadown 11E6
Seafield 11F4
Seaford 8D1
Seaforth 11E6
Seaview 10A2
Seaward Downs........15C4
Seddon 8H5
Seddonville 8B5
Sedgemere 10E6
Sefton.......................10F4
Selwyn Huts 10E6
Selwyn 10E5
Selwyn 3E3
Sentry Hill 5B2
Sergeants Hill.............8A6
Shaftesbury...............3D2
Shag Point 13G5

Shag Valley 13F4
Shannon....................13E5
Shannon.....................7D2
Shantytown 10B1
Sheffield....................10D4
Shelly Beach.............2C4
Shenandoah 8C6
Sherenden 6D4
Sherwood Downs.......11D4
Silverdale 2D4
Silverhope 5F6
Six Mile 8C6
Skippers 13A2
Slaty Creek 9A3
Slope Point...............15D5
Snells Beach..............2D3
South Bay 9G3
South Beach 10B1
South Head 2C3
South Hillend 15B3
South Malvern...........10D5
Southbridge 10E6
Southbrook................10E4
Southburn 11D6
Spar Bush................15B4
Speargrass Flat..........13A3
Spencerville 10F5
Spotswood 9F5
Spring Creek............8G5
Spring Grove 8E4
Springbank 10E4
Springbrook 13G1
Springdale................3D2
Springfield.................10D4
Springfield.................2C1
Springhill...................5H5
Springhills 15C3
Springs Flat..............1F6
Springs Junction 9C3
Springston South 10E6
Springston.................10E5
Springvale 13C4
Spye 9E6
St Andrews 13G1
St Arnaud..................8D6
St Bathans 13D2
St Omer 8G3
St Patricks 13A6
Stafford 10B2
Staircase..................10D4
Stanley Brook 8D4
Stanmore Bay 2D4
Stanway....................5F6
Stavely......................10C5
Stewarts Gully 10F4
Stillwater 2D4

Stillwater 9A4
Stirling 15F4
Stockton 8B5
Stoke.........................8E4
Stokes Valley.............7C5
Stoneburn.................13F4
Stony Creek 15F3
Stratford 5B3
Strathmore 5C3
Streamlands..............2D3
Struan 13F1
Studholme 13G2
Summer Hill...............15F4
Summerhill 10E4
Summerlands 8F5
Summerlea................8B5
Sumner......................10F5
Surfdale....................2E5
Sutherlands 11D6
Sutton.......................13E5
Swannanoa 10E4
Swanson 2D5
Sweetwater 1C3

T
Table Hill...................15F3
Tablelands.................4E3
Tablelands.................7E5
Tadmore....................8D4
Taemaro 1D3
Tahaia 3C5
Tahakopa 15E5
Taharoa 3A4
Tahatika....................15E4
Tahawai 3E2
Taheke 1D5
Tahekeroa 2D4
Tahere 1F6
Tahora 3H5
Tahora 5D2
Tahoraiti....................7F1
Tahuna 3D2
Tahunanui 8E4
Tahunga 4E6
Tahuroa 3D2
Taieri Beach..............15G3
Taieri Mouth 15G3
Taihape......................5F4
Taiharuru 1G6
Taihoa 3D3
Taikirau 1E5
Taikorea 7D1
Taimate 8H6
Taingaehe 2B2
Taipa 1D3
Taipoiti......................9B2

Taipuha 2C1
Tairua.......................2G5
Taitapu 10E5
Takahiwai 1F6
Takahue 1C4
Takaka 8D2
Takamatua.................10F6
Takamore 4G3
Takapau 4G3
Takapau 4G5
Takapau 5H6
Takapuna 2D4
Takaputahi.................4E4
Takatu 2D3
Takou bay 1E4
Takutai......................10A2
Tamahere 3C3
Tamaterau 1F6
Tamihana 3D3
Tanatana 3H4
Tane 7E2
Taneatua 3H4
Tanehopuwai..............3C5
Tanekaha...................1F5
Tangihua....................1F6
Tangimoana 7D1
Tangiteroria 1E6
Tangitu......................3C6
Tangiwai 5F4
Tangoio 6E3
Tangowahine 2B1
Taniwha.....................3C1
Tanoa 2C2
Taonui.......................7E1
Taoroa Junction 5G5
Taotaoroa..................3D3
Tapanui 15D2
Tapapa 3E4
Tapawera 8D4
Tapora 2C3
Tapu 2F5
Tapuhi.......................1F5
Tapui.........................13F3
Tapuwae 1D4
Tapuwae 3C6
Tara 2D2
Taradale 6E4
Tarakohe 8D2
Taramakau 9A5
Taramoa 15B4
Taranui......................13G3
Tarapatiki...................6F1
Tarara 15E5
Tararu 2F6
Tarata 5B2
Taraunui.....................1G6

Tarawera

Tarawera	6D2	Te Akatarewa	13E1
Tariki	5B3	Te Akau South	3B2
Taringamotu Valley	5E1	Te Akau	3B2
Taringamotu	5E1	Te Anau Downs	14E2
Taronui Bay	1E4	Te Anau	14E3
Tarras	13C2	Te Anga	3B5
Tarukenga	3E4	Te Arai Point	2D2
Tarurutangi	5B2	Te Arai	2D2
Tasman	8E4	Te Arakura	7E1
Tataiahape	3H4	Te Araroa	4H2
Tatapouri	4G6	Te Ariruru	4G4
Tataraimaka	5A2	Te Aroha West	3D2
Tataramoa	5G6	Te Aroha	3D2
Tatare	11B2	Te Awa	11E5
Tatariki	2B2	Te Awamutu	3C4
Tatu	5D2	Te Awanga	6E4
Tatuanui	3D2	Te Hana	2D2
Tauhei	3C2	Te Hapua	1B1
Tauherenikau	7D4	Te Haroto	6D2
Tauhoa	2C3	Te Hauke	6E5
Taumarere	1E5	Te Henga	2C5
Taumarunui	5E1	Te Hihi	2D6
Taumata	15E3	Te Hoe	3C2
Taumutu	10E6	Te Horo Beach	7C3
Taupaki	2D5	Te Horo	7C3
Taupiri	3C2	Te Houka	15E3
Taupo Bay	1D3	Te Huahua	1D4
Taupo	3E6	Te Hutewai	3B3
Tauranga Bay	1E3	Te Iringa	1E5
Tauranga Valley	1E3	Te Kaha	4F2
Tauranga	3E2	Te Kao	1B2
Tauranganui	3B1	Te Karae	1D4
Taurangaruru	2D6	Te Karaka	1D5
Tauraroa	2C1	Te Karaka	4F5
Taurewa	5F2	Te Kauri	3C2
Tauriko	3E3	Te Kauwhata	3C1
Taurikura	1G6	Te Kawa West	3C4
Tautoro	1E5	Te Kawa	3C4
Tauweru	7E4	Te Kinga	9A4
Tauwhare Pa	3C3	Te Kiri	5A3
Tauwhare	3C3	Te Kohanga	3B1
Tauwhare	3H5	Te Kopua	3C4
Tauwhareparae	4G4	Te Kopua	4F2
Tawa	7C4	Te Kopuru	2B2
Tawai	13G2	Te Koraha	3B4
Tawanui	15E4	Te Kowhai	3C3
Tawataia	7E2	Te Kuha	8A6
Tawhai	9B2	Te Kuiti	3C5
Tawhana	3H5	Te Kumi	3C5
Tawharanui	2D3	Te Mahia	8G4
Tawharemanuka	3H5	Te Mahoe	3G4
Tawhata	5D2	Te Maire	5E2
Tawhiti	5B4	Te Mapara	3B5
Taylors Mistake	10F5	Te Mata	2F5
Taylorville	9A4	Te Mata	3B3
Te Ahuahu	1E4	Te Matai	3F3

Te Mawhai	3C4	Te Whaiti	3G6
Te Miko	9A2	Te Whakarae	5E2
Te Miro	3D3	Te Whanga	7E4
Te Moana	11D5	Te Wharau	2B1
Te Moananui	3D1	Te Wharau	7E5
Te Namu	8B4	Tekapo Military Camp	11C5
Te Ngae	3F4	Temple View	3C3
Te Ngaire	1E3	Templeton	10E5
Te Ohaki Pa	3E3	Temuka	11E6
Te Ore Ore	7E4	Tennyson Inlet	8G3
Te Pahu	3C3	Teschemakers	13G3
Te Paki	1B1	Teviot	13C5
Te Papatapu	3B3	Thames	2F6
Te Peka	15D5	The Branch	8E5
Te Pene	1E3	The Five Bridges	4G5
Te Perita	10D5	The Forks	11B2
Te Pohue	6E3	The Grove	8G4
Te Poi	3E3	The Kaik	10F6
Te Popo	5B3	The Key	15A1
Te Pua	2C4	The Peaks	9D5
Te Puia Springs	4G4	The Pines Beach	10F4
Te Puka	4G4	The Point	10C5
Te Puke	3F3	The Rocks	15B4
Te Puna	3E2	Thompsons Crossing	15B3
Te Puninga	3D2	Thornbury	15B4
Te Puru	2F6	Thornton Bay	2F6
Te Rae	8D1	Thornton	3G3
Te Rahu	3C3	Thorpe	8D4
Te Ranga	3E3	Three Bridges	1D5
Te Ranga	3F3	Three Mile Bush	1F6
Te Rangiita	5G1	Ti Point	2D3
Te Rapa Stn	9H1	Ti Tree Point	7G2
Te Rapa	3C3	Tiakitahuna	7E2
Te Rauamoa	3B4	Tihiroa	3C4
Te Raumauku	3C4	Tihoi	3D6
Te Raupo	1C2	Tikinui	2B2
Te Reinga	6G1	Tikitere	3F4
Te Rerenga	2G4	Tikitiki	4H3
Te Rore	1C4	Tikokino	5H5
Te Rore	3C3	Tikorangi	5B2
Te Roti	5B4	Tikotiko	3B2
Te Rou	8F5	Timaru	11E6
Te Taho	11C2	Timber Bay	7F1
Te Teko	3G4	Timpanys	15C4
Te Tii	1E4	Tiniroto	4E6
Te Tipua	15C3	Tinopai	2C2
Te Toro	2D6	Tinui	7F3
Te Tua	14E5	Tinwald	11F4
Te Tuhi Junction	5D4	Tipapakuku	7F1
Te Tumu	3F3	Tiratu	7F1
Te Uku	3B3	Tirau	3D3
Te Uri	7G1	Tiraumea	7F2
Te Waewae	14E6	Tiriraukawa	5F5
Te Waiiti	3H6	Tiroa	3C6
Te Wairoa	3F4	Tirohanga	15F4
Te Wera	5C3	Tirohanga	4E3

Tirohanga

Tirohia

Tirohia	3D1
Tiroiti	13E4
Tiromoana	9A2
Tiroroa	8B6
Tisbury	15B4
Titahi Bay	7C4
Titirangi Bay	8H3
Titirangi	2D5
Titiroa	15C5
Titoki	1E6
Titri	15G3
Toatoa	4E4
Tohunga Junction	5E3
Toi Flat	7G1
Toiro	15E4
Tokaanu	5F2
Tokanui	15D5
Tokanui	3C4
Tokaora	5B4
Tokata	4G2
Tokatoka	2B2
Tokerau Beach	1C3
Tokirima	5D2
Toko Mouth	15F3
Toko	5C3
Tokoiti	15F3
Tokomaru Bay	4G4
Tokomaru	7E2
Tokorahi	13F3
Tokorangi	5E6
Tokoroa	3E4
Tolaga Bay	4G5
Tomarata	2D2
Tongaporutu	5C1
Tongariro	5F2
Tophouse	8D6
Topuni	2C2
Torehape	3C1
Torere	4E3
Tormore	9F5
Totara Flat	9A3
Totara North	1D3
Totara Valley	11D6
Totara	13G3
Totara	2F6
Totaranui	8E2
Towai	1F5
Trentham	7C4
Trentham	11D5
Tripp Settlement	11E5
Tryphena	2F3
Tuahiwi	10F4
Tuai	6F1
Tuakau	2E6
Tuamarina	8G4
Tuapeka Flat	15E2

Tuapeka Mouth	15E3
Tuapeka West	15E2
Tuatapere	14E5
Tuateawa	2G4
Tuatini	4G4
Tuhara	6G2
Tuhikaramea	3C3
Tuhipa	1E5
Tuhitarata	7D5
Tuhua	5E1
Tui Glen	8F4
Tui	8D5
Tukemokihi	6G2
Tumahu	5A3
Tumai	13F5
Tumunui	3F5
Tuna	5B3
Tunakotekote	5E1
Tuparoa	4H3
Turakina	5E6
Turangaomoana	3E3
Turangarere	5F4
Turangi	5F2
Turitea	7E2
Turiwhate	9A5
Turiwiri	2B1
Turua	2F6
Tussock Creek	15B4
Tutaematai	1F4
Tutaenui	5E6
Tutaki	8C6
Tutamoe	1D6
Tutekehua	1D4
Tutira	6E3
Tutukaka	1G6
Tuturau	15D4
Tuturumuri	7D5
Tututawa	5C3
Twin Bridges	1E6
Twizel	11B6
Twyford	6E4
Tyntesfield	8G5

U

Umawera	1D4
Umere	8C4
Umukuri	8E3
Umutaoroa	5G6
Umutoi	5G6
Unahi	1C3
Underwood	15B4
Upokongaro	5D5
Upokorau	1E4
Upper Atiamuri	3E
Upper Hutt	7C4
Upper Junction	13F6

Upper Kawhatau	5G5
Upper Matikitaki	9D2
Upper Moutere	8E4
Upper Retaruke	5E2
Upper Takaka	8D3
Upper Waitati	13F6
Upper Waitohi	11E5
Urenui	5C2
Uretane	13G2
Urquharts Bay	2D1
Urungaio	1D4
Uruti	5C2
Uruwhenua	8D3
Utakura	1D4
Utiku	5F5
Utuwai	5G6

V

Valletta	10C6
Victoria Valley	1D4
View Hill	10D4
Vinegar Hill	5F5

W

Waddington	10D4
Waenga	13C3
Waerenga	3C1
Waerengaahika	4F6
Waerengaokuri	4F6
Waharoa	3D3
Waianakarua	13F4
Waianiwa	15B4
Waiapi	11E6
Waiare	1E4
Waiariari	13G1
Waiarikiki	15D4
Waiaro	2F4
Waiaruhe	7F1
Waiatarua	2D5
Waiatoto	12E3
Waiau Beach	2D6
Waiau Pa	2D6
Waiau	9E4
Waiaua	4E3
Waihaha	1F4
Waihana	15D4
Waihao Downs	13G2
Waihao Forks	13G2
Waihaorunga	13G2
Waihapa	1D3
Waiharakeke	3E1
Waiharara	1C3
Waihau Bay	4F2
Waihi Beach	3E1
Waihi Gorge	11E5
Waihi	3E1

Waimangu

Waihi	5F2
Waihirere	4F6
Waihoaka	14E6
Waihoki Valley	7F3
Waihoki	7F2
Waihola	15F3
Waihopo	1C2
Waihou Valley	1D4
Waihou	3D2
Waihua	6F2
Waihue	1E6
Waiinu Beach	5C5
Wai-iti	8E4
Waikaia	13B6
Waikaka Valley	15D3
Waikaka	15D2
Waikakahi	13G2
Waikanae Beach	7C3
Waikanae	7C3
Waikaraka	1F6
Waikaremoana	6F1
Waikaretu	3B2
Waikari	9D6
Waikato	8D1
Waikaura	13F2
Waikawa Beach	7D3
Waikawa Valley	15D5
Waikawa	15D5
Waikawa	8G4
Waikawau	2F4
Waikawau	2F5
Waikawau	3A5
Waikiekie	2C1
Waikino	3D1
Waikirikiri	3H5
Waikite Valley	3F5
Waikoau	6E3
Waikoikoi	15D3
Waikokopu	6H2
Waikokowai	3B2
Waikorea	3B2
Waikouaiti	13F5
Waikoukou Valley	2D4
Waikouro	15A3
Waikuku Beach	10F4
Waikuku	10F4
Waikune	5E3
Waima Valley	1D5
Waima	1D5
Waima	4G4
Waimahaka	15C5
Waimahora	3C5
Waimamaku	1D5
Waimana	3H4
Waimangaroa	8B6
Waimangu	3F5

Waimanoni	1C3	Waipaoa	4F5	Waitao	3F3
Waimapu	3E3	Waipapa	1E4	Waitapu	1C5
Waimarama	6F5	Waipapakauri Beach	1C3	Waitapu	8D2
Waimarie	8B5	Waipapakauri	1C3	Waitara	5B2
Waimata	3E1	Waipara	9E6	Waitarere	7D2
Waimata	4F5	Waiparera	1G6	Waitaria Bay	8G3
Waimate North	1E4	Waiparu	13B6	Waitaruke	1D3
Waimate	13G2	Waipatiki Beach	6F3	Waitati	13F6
Waimatenui	1D6	Waipatiki	7G1	Waitawa	11E6
Waimatua	15C5	Waipawa	5H6	Waitawheta	3D1
Waimatuku	15B4	Waipiata	13E4	Waiteitei	2D3
Waimauku	2C4	Waipipi	2D6	Waitekauri	3D1
Waimaunga	9B3	Waipiro Bay	4G4	Waitepeka	15E4
Waimiha	3C6	Waipopo	11E6	Waiterimu	3C2
Waimiro	7F2	Waipori Falls	13E6	Waiteti	3F4
Waimotu	13G3	Waipoua Forest	1D6	Waitetoki	1D3
Waimumu	15C3	Waipoua Settlement	1D6	Waitetoko	5G2
Waingake	6H1	Waipounamu	13B6	Waitetuna	3B3
Waingarara	3H4	Waipu Caves	2C1	Waiti	3D2
Waingaro	3B2	Waipu Cove	2D2	Waitiki Landing	1B1
Waingawa	7E4	Waipu	2C1	Waitiri	13B3
Wainihinihi	9A5	Waipuku	5B3	Waitoa	3D2
Wainui Junction	1C4	Waipukurau	6D6	Waitoetoe	5C2
Wainui Junction	5F4	Waipuna	9A3	Waitohi	11E5
Wainui	10F6	Wairakau	3D2	Waitohi	7D1
Wainui	1E3	Wairakei Village	3E6	Waitoki	2D4
Wainui	2D4	Wairakei	3E6	Waitomo Caves	3B5
Wainui	3H4	Wairamarama	3B1	Waitomo Valley	3C4
Wainui	4G6	Wairata	4E4	Waitoriki	5B2
Wainuiomata	7C5	Wairau Bar	8G5	Waitotara	5C5
Wainuioru	7E4	Wairau Valley	8F5	Waituhi	4F6
Waioeka Pa	4E4	Waireia	1C5	Waitui	5B2
Waiohau	3G5	Waireka	3E5	Waituna West	5F6
Waiomatatini	4H3	Wairere	2C2	Waituna	13G2
Waiomio	1E5	Wairio	15A3	Waituna	15C4
Waiomu	2F5	Wairoa Pa	3E2	Waiuku	2D6
Waione	7G2	Wairoa	3E3	Waiuta	9B3
Waioneke	2C4	Wairoa	4H3	Waiwaka	7E3
Waiongana	5B2	Wairoa	6G2	Waiwera South	15E3
Waiorongomai	3D2	Wairuna	15E3	Waiwera	2D4
Waiorore	4F2	Wairunga	13F5	Waiwera	7E2
Waiotahi Beach	4D3	Waitaanga	5D1	Waiwhare	5H4
Waiotahi Pa	3H4	Waitaha	10A3	Waiwhiu	2D3
Waiotahi Valley	3H4	Waitahanui	5G1	Wakanui	11F4
Waiotahi	3H4	Waitahora	7F1	Wakapatu	15A4
Waiotama	1E6	Waitahu	9B2	Wakapuaka	8F4
Waiotapu	3F5	Waitahuna Gully	15F3	Wakarara	5G5
Waiotehue	1C4	Waitahuna West	15E3	Wakare	1F4
Waiotemarama	1D5	Waitahuna	15F3	Wakefield	8E4
Waiotira	2C1	Waitakaruru	2F6	Waldronville	15G2
Waiotu	1F5	Waitakere	2D5	Wallacetown	15B4
Waiouru	5F4	Waitaki	13G2	Wallingford	7G1
Waipa Valley	3C5	Waitane	15C3	Walter Peak Stn	13A3
Waipahi	15D3	Waitangi	13E1	Walton	3D3
Waipaipai	1F5	Waitangi	1E4	Wamatenui	1D6
Waipango	15A4	Waitanguru	3B5	Wanaka	13B2

Wangaloa	15F4
Wanganui	5D5
Wanstead	5H6
Waotu	3D4
Ward	8H6
Wardville	3D2
Warea	5A3
Warepa	15E4
Warkworth	2D3
Warrington	13F6
Washdyke	11E6
Waterton	11F5
Wattle Bay	2D5
Wattle Downs	2E6
Waverly	5C5
Wayby Valley	2D3
Wayby	2D3
Weavers Crossing	3C2
Weber	7G2
Wedderburn	13E3
Weedons	10E5
Weka Pass	9D6
Wekaweka	1D5
Welcome Bay	3F3
Welds Hill Stn	9G1
Wellington	7B5
Wellsford	2D3
Wendon Valley	13B6
Wendon	13B6
Wendonside	13B6
West Eyreton	10E4
West Melton	10E5
West Plains	15B4
West Wanaka	13B1
Westerfield	10C6
Westmere	3C2
Westmere	5D5
Weston	13G3
Westport	8A6
Westshore	6E4
Wetheral	10E4
Wetherston	13D6
Weymouth	2D6
Whakaangiangi	4G2
Whakaki	6G2
Whakamara	5C4
Whakamarama	3E3
Whakamaru	3D5
Whakapapa Village	5F3
Whakapara	1F5
Whakapirau	2C2
Whakapourangi	4G3
Whakarae	3H5
Whakarewarewa	3F4
Whakarongo	7E1
Whakatane	3H4

Whakatete Bay   **Yaldhurst**

Whakatete Bay 2F6
Whakatiwai 2F6
Whakatu.....................6E4
Whakawhitira 4G3
Whananaki South 1G5
Whananaki 1F5
Whanarua Bay 4F2
Whanawhana..............5H4
Whangae....................1E4
Whangaehu 5D6
Whangaimoana...........7D5
Whangamarino 3C1
Whangamarino............3F4
Whangamata 2G6
Whangamoa................8F3
Whangamomona 5C2
Whangaparaoa 2D4
Whangaparaoa 4G2
Whangaparapara 2F2
Whangape 1C4
Whangapoua 2G4
Whangara 4G6
Whangarata 2E6
Whangarei Heads........1G6
Whangarei..................1F6
Whangaripo 2D3
Whangaroa 1E3
Whangaruru North 1F4
Whangaruru South.......1F5
Whangaruru 1F4
Whangateau 2D3
Wharanui 8H6
Whare Flat.................13F6
Whareama...................7F4

Wharehine 2C3
Wharehuanui..............13A3
Wharehuia..................5B3
Wharekaka 4G5
Wharekauhau 7C5
Wharekawa 2F6
Wharekawa..................2G6
Wharekohe..................1E6
Wharekopae................4E5
Whareora 1F6
Wharepapa South........3D4
Wharepapa 2C4
Wharepoa 3D1
Whareponga 4H3
Wharepuhunga 3D4
Whareroa 5B4
Whareroa 5F1
Wharetoa 15E3
Wharewaka.................5G1
Wharua.....................13F2
Whataroa 11B2
Whatataki 7F3
Whatatutu 4F5
Whatawhata................3C3
Whatipu.....................2C5
Whatitiri 1F6
Whatoro 1D6
Whatuwhiwhi...............1D3
Whawharua.................3C5
Wheatstone 11F5
Wheki Valley...............1F6
Whenuahou 5H6
Whenuakite.................2G5
Whenuakura 5C5

Whenuanui..................2B2
Whenuapai.................2D5
Whetukura 5H6
Whirinaki....................1D5
Whirinaki 6E3
Whiritoa......................3E1
Whiriwhiri 2D6
White Pine Bush 3H4
White Rock 9D6
Whitecliffs 10D5
Whitehall 3D3
Whiterigg..................15D3
Whitford....................2E5
Whitianga...................2G5
Whitianga 4E3
Whitikahu...................3C2
Whitikau 4E4
Whitstone.................13G3
Wilden.....................13C6
Wilder Settlement 7G1
Willow Flat..................6F2
Willowbank...............15D3
Willowbridge 13G2
Willowby 11F4
Willowford 5H4
Wilsons Crossing 15B4
Wilsonville 1F5
Wiltsdown 3D4
Wimbledon.................7G2
Winchester...............10C6
Winchester 11E5
Windermere 11F4
Windsor Park 13G3
Windsor.....................13F3

Windwhistle...............10C5
Windy Hill 2B1
Wingatui 13F6
Winiata 5F5
Winscombe 11D5
Winslow....................11F4
Winton......................15B3
Woodbourne 8G5
Woodbury.................11E5
Woodcocks 2D3
Woodend Beach........10F4
Woodend...................10F4
Woodend..................15B5
Woodhill 2C4
Woodlands 15C4
Woodlands 3E2
Woodlands 4D3
Woodlaw 15A3
Woodleigh 3B2
Woodside 13E6
Woodstock 10A2
Woodstock 8D4
Woodville...................7F1
Woolleys Bay 1G5
Wreys Bush...............15B3
Wrights Bush............15B4
Wylies Crossing 13E6
Wyndham..................15C4

Y

Yaldhurst 10E5

ISBN 1-86958-791-X

©1999 New Zealand Automobile Association Inc
The moral rights of the author have been asserted.

First published in 1994 by Moa Beckett Publishers Limited

Published by Hodder Moa Beckett Publishers Limited
4 Whetu Place, Mairangi Bay, Auckland, New Zealand

Revised edition 1999
Reprinted 1995 (three times) & 1996 (revised edition), reprinted 1997, 1998, 1999

Land Information New Zealand Licence PL 097046/110

Printed by Bookprint International, Hong Kong